STAYING FREELANCE

STAYING
FREELANCE

HOW I ACHIEVED LASTING SUCCESS AS A BOOK PUBLISHING PROFESSIONAL

ANDREA REIDER

Gold Letter Press

Gold Letter Press
West Hollywood, CA 90069
goldletterpress1@gmail.com

ISBN: 979-8-218-49027-0

Dedicated to my beloved grandparents,
Ruth and Julius Olen

CONTENTS

Preface   ix

Introduction   1

PART ONE
STARTING OUT AS A FREELANCER

Chapter 1   Getting Paid to Learn Desktop Publishing   7
Chapter 2   Working as a Freelance Book Typesetter   17
Chapter 3   Everything Keeps Changing   25
Chapter 4   Becoming a Freelance Book Typesetter   45
Chapter 5   Keeping Busy as a Freelancer   67

PART TWO
THE SEARCH FOR NEW
CLIENTS GOES ON

Chapter 6   Leaving San Francisco   95
Chapter 7   Shutting It All Down   107
Chapter 8   Business Building Never Ends   127
Chapter 9   Maintaining a Freelance Business   143

Conclusion   157

APPENDIX
INTERIOR BOOK DESIGNS

Classic Books: Interior Pages   161

About the Author   173

PREFACE

Going freelance is one thing, but my book is called *Staying Freelance* because it is about the many things I did to start, grow, and maintain my freelance business over the course of almost forty years as a book design and typesetting professional. I've worked on thousands of books for other authors and finally the time came for me to write my own book.

When I decided to write this book, I thought it would be a nonfiction book about freelancing, with facts and statistics, and helpful advice for people considering a such a career. But as I continued writing, I began to see that my own story of building my freelance book design and typesetting business might be interesting and instructive to others considering their own freelance careers.

Much of my story as a book design and typesetting freelancer since the late 1980s is about the constant struggle and the ongoing efforts required to find new customers and maintain relationships with existing ones. I've tried to detail the many and varied things I did in my attempts to keep growing my client base. Some of the things that failed for me might end up working for you.

I advise anyone seeking to establish a full-time freelance career in any profession, or even just part-time to supplement income, to use your creativity and ingenuity to figure out ways to focus on reaching out to other businesses and individuals who might be in need of your services. You really don't know what types of opportunities are out there until you start making contact with potential clients.

I've built my business primarily through using cold-call letters and emails to reach out to thousands of other book publishing professionals employed by publishers, or working on their own like me. Most of my success has come from sending out enough mailings to sometimes contact the right person or business at just the right time.

Although I might only hear back from a few people out of one hundred or more emails, most people that do write back thank me for reaching out to them. Some write back to tell me that they already are working with another freelancer or are doing the work in-house, but many responses lead to real freelance work—sometimes just a single project, but often leading to work on a long-term basis.

While learning to find new clients is an essential skill for all freelancers, I have been successful for so many years because I took the time and effort required to become an expert in my field. For me, it helped to narrow my focus by specializing in book design and layout, a sub-specialty in the broader field of graphic design.

At the beginning of my freelance career I worked on graphic design projects for many types of large and small companies in San Francisco. But my business really took off when I decided to focus all of my efforts toward working exclusively as a designer and typesetter for book publishers. This cut out a lot of potential clients that I could approach for freelance work, but it allowed me to focus like a laser beam on book publishing, and develop my own expertise in the field.

I've loved everything about the art and practice of book design and typesetting from the moment I started working on my first books. But my love of books would never have been enough to carry me through a lifelong career—or even to get me in the door of most publishers. I had to learn everything that I could about book design and layout—while always keeping current with the latest computer developments and software releases.

Mostly through experience working on book projects and learning from my colleagues and peers, I set about building myself into the best designer and typesetter that

I could be, so that authors, editors, and publishers would want to work with me as much as I wanted to work with them.

In my many years of experience, book publishers have been more or less open to my approaches as a new freelancer, but most publishers already have their needs met by other freelancers and businesses with whom they have long-term working relationships. Something has to be changing at the company for a book publisher to be open to working with me as a new freelancer. I've gotten some of my best clients over the years when other free-lancers have had to leave their jobs due to illness or just reaching retirement age, opening up a new position for me.

I've been promoting my freelance business for decades without spending much money on traditional forms of advertisement beyond boosting some online posts and placing the occasional advertisement on some book publishing sites. I've built dozens of long-term relationships with book publishing clients by sending prospective clients a cover letter, resume, and samples of my work. My biggest expenses used to be paper and stamps, until I began reaching out to new clients exclu-sively through email.

I think some publishers appreciated receiving my printed samples through the mail. But just being able to click "respond" to my emails made it easier for people to get back to me. And I can send out a lot more letters via email than I could ever have done using the U.S. mail.

It's always best to find the names and email addresses of the person at the company who is in charge of hiring freelancers. If I can't find that information, I'll just send an email to the general information email address, and hope that it makes it to the right person or department. I've found many clients through this method and find that it's always worth a try.

To promote my book design and typesetting freelance business I search for things such as,"book publishing editor," "managing editor," "publishing manager," "book production editor," and just about any other combination of terms that I can come up with.

As I was writing this book, it was a little overwhelming for me to realize just how many clients I have gained and lost over the years. Fortunately, the many good working relationships and experiences I've had with authors and publishers far outweigh the unavoidable problems that arise when working on projects with highly demanding book publisher clients. It can be even more difficult working with self-publishing authors who are not familiar with the publishing process and can be very demanding in many ways.

When I look back on my long career as a freelance book designer and typesetter, what really stands out to me is the constant struggle to attract enough work to keep myself as busy as I wanted and needed to be. I was always under pressure to maintain a relatively high income because I was living in San Francisco and then Los Angeles, where the cost of living is so high.

It might have been easier for me if I had been operating my home-based business in a less expensive place. However, I made many book publishing contacts because I was living in San Francisco, which had a very vibrant publishing community in the city and greater area.

For the first twenty years of my freelancing career, I worked almost exclusively with book publishers. I had very little or no contact at all with the authors of the books I worked on. The production editors who managed the book projects always treated me very well and did their best to shield me from most of the inevitable problems and issues that can arise when working on a book from design and typesetting through to printed books.

While some authors have a lot of control over the editing and proofreading of their books, most editors and publishers try to place limits on the number of changes that authors can make to their own books once they have gone through editing and arrived at the design and typesetting stage. Nonetheless, a significant part of my income comes from making author and editorial changes to the book text and formatting after I've done the initial complete design and layout. Some books can go through over a dozen rounds of revisions before the production editor in charge of the project is satisfied that the book is ready to be printed.

One of the many things that has kept me happy as a freelancer for so many years is that the vast majority of my clients have been and continue to be very kind and respectful toward me. The "Great job!" and "Thanks for your wonderful work!" comments are always most welcome and continue to keep me encouraged and engaged with my work.

When I was first getting started as a freelancer, a little praise went a long way and was extremely helpful in building up my confidence in my abilities and career path. The kindness of others was a big factor in helping me to keep working as a freelancer long enough to develop the skills and expertise that I would continue to hone over a lifetime.

I hope that reading about my experience as a career freelancer will inspire others to pursue their own dreams and see where their efforts can take them. I would advise you to be prepared for some failures along the way, and then to pick yourself up and turn all adversities into future successes.

The struggle was well worth it for me. I derive a great deal of satisfaction and much joy from my work. It gives meaning and structure to my life, and I take great pride in a job well done. Helping authors to bring their books to life is very rewarding for me, and I place a high value on the many relationships that I've built with colleagues and clients.

INTRODUCTION

graduated from the University of Michigan in 1985 with a B.A. in English. I was an avid reader of classic literature as a young person, and loved nothing more than reading and re-reading a long and challenging book.

I grew up in the suburbs of Detroit, about a forty-minute drive from the University of Michigan in Ann Arbor, and had absolutely no desire to stray far from home. But my young world was turned upside down when my parents decided to move to San Francisco while I was a sophomore at college. I didn't want to leave behind everyone and everything that I knew and loved to move to San Francisco, so I decided to stay in Ann Arbor, finish school, get a job, and try to make it on my own.

The Apple Macintosh computer had just recently been introduced and was starting to gain popularity. Among many other things, the new and affordable desktop computers enabled what became known as "desktop publishing," which was a new and exciting field at the time.

After I graduated, I found my first job managing a small typesetting shop in Ann Arbor that was transitioning from using expensive computer typesetting equipment to the relatively low-cost Macintosh computers and desktop publishing software. I quickly learned how to use the Microsoft Word version 1 software to typeset resumes, reports, and even one book. Our customers included University of Michigan students and professors as well as local businesses and individuals of every description.

I got the job after a preliminary interview and test that included a section where I had to match typefaces to their names. I don't know how well I scored on the test, but I was soon on my way to being completely fascinated by everything having to do with typesetting and page layout.

My parents didn't understand when I told them that the world was at the beginning of a revolution in publishing, and that I was learning useful and marketable skills at the typesetting shop. They encouraged me to find an entry-level job at a big corporation as many of my peers were doing at the time. That path had little appeal for me, but I did spend some time studying for the LSAT law school entrance exams—which seemed to be a reasonable path forward for me.

I learned a lot about how to use the Macintosh computers and early versions of Microsoft Word and Aldus

PageMaker, but I hadn't learned much about how to be a graphic designer during my time at the typesetting shop in Ann Arbor. It was easier to please clients back then, and most people thought that it was "amazing" that we could do what amounted to just basic formatting and layouts for them on the new computers.

I stayed in Ann Arbor for two years after I graduated, but I always wanted to live close to my parents and brother and sister, who were all now living in San Francisco. I had no idea what I would do for work when I got there, and soon found myself living with my parents and very anxious to move into my own apartment.

My very first job as a young person had been working at my family's men's clothing store in the suburbs of Detroit, Michigan. The store was originally located in downtown Detroit on a street known as the "Avenue of Fashion," and had been in business for fifty years when my father decided to close the store and move to San Francisco.

I loved everything about working at the store, known as Block's Clothes, and as a child always imagined that one day I would be in charge of the store. My grandfather, who had founded the store, once told me that I worked harder "than any boy" that had ever worked for him. I considered that to be high praise, considering the source, and tried to work even harder, faster, and better at my many tasks and responsibilities at the store.

My favorite job as the self-appointed department manager of the stockroom, was putting the price tags on the clothing as it arrived in the stock room, which was located against one wall in the tailor shop in the back of the store. The price tags came out of a 1980s state-of-the-art Pitney Bowes pin-ticketing machine, which printed out the retail price, the wholesale cost (set in code), and the size of the garment printed on the tags. I consider this to have been my first typesetting job.

The only real full-time job that I had ever applied for was at the typesetting shop in Ann Arbor—everyone in my family worked at the clothing store, so that hardly counted as getting a job. I hadn't even decided on a career path yet, and was still thinking about law school as a way out of my financial dilemma.

One of the first stops I made in my job search was at a temporary employment agency located in San Francisco's business district. It came as a happy surprise that my early Macintosh typesetting experience had taught me some very desirable skills that many employers were now looking for. I was at the right place at the right time and had no trouble finding work that I enjoyed, and that paid me more than I realized or even thought I was worth at the time.

STARTING OUT AS A FREELANCER

CHAPTER 1

GETTING PAID TO LEARN DESKTOP PUBLISHING

A temporary employment agency placed me in my first job in San Francisco, working in the downtown headquarters of a large manufacturing company. I was hired as part of a test to see whether they should invest in new Macintosh desktop publishing equipment or go with the IBM PC equivalent.

My job was to use the Macintosh computer to lay out a large manual using the popular layout program Aldus PageMaker. Another woman was hired to work on an IBM computer using the page layout program Ventura Graphics.

At this time, the Macintosh computer and the Aldus PageMaker were much better suited to desktop publishing applications and eventually came to dominate in the graphic design industry. The advantage of working on the better desktop publishing system and my experience from working at the typesetting shop in Ann Arbor enabled me to finish my project in about a week. My IBM PC competitor on Ventura Graphics was still working on her project six weeks later.

I found out later that the other woman had been the favorite of most of the secretaries at the company, and that they had all been rooting for her to beat me. My winning the competition meant that I was hired to help the company to develop their in-house desktop publishing department using Macintosh computers.

I started out making $14 per hour as a temporary worker, which was an decent wage in 1987. After making myself very useful and with some bargaining, the company bought out my contract with the temporary agency, and agreed to pay me $20 per hour, which they ultimately raised to $25 per hour. Although consultants in other fields were then charging as much as $50 to $100 per hour and more for their services, I was now making enough steady money to be enable me to move out of my parents' house and into my first San Francisco apartment.

I found a cute and tiny studio apartment in the Nob Hill district, two blocks from the Fairmont Hotel. It was within walking distance to my favorite hangout, the Caffe Trieste in North Beach. This was a big plus to me at the time, as the Caffe had become the center of my social life outside of my work and family.

There was always something to do when I was working at our family men's clothing store in Detroit, even if it meant vacuuming the carpet, making coffee, or just straightening up the merchandise on display. My father used to tell me that I was working too fast, warning me that people might take advantage of me one day for working too hard. The pace was always hectic and pressured at the typesetting shop in Ann Arbor. There was always more work to do then there were hours in the day.

The pace at the manufacturing company's office was nothing like what I had experienced working for small businesses, and seemed to be like slow motion in comparison. At first, I didn't have nearly enough work to do to fill the day, so I spent my time trying to focus on learning more about how to use the Macintosh computer and software. I spent many hours experimenting with the various programs installed on the computer, just seeing what I could come up with as I sat in my office waiting for the next piece of work to come in.

Ultimately, more and more people in the office became aware of the desktop publishing services that I could provide, and I found myself working hard enough to have a good sense of accomplishment at the end of most days. I worked on a variety of corporate communication: slide shows for presentations, all types of reports, reviews, and manuals—and whatever else they could think of to throw my way. I enjoyed working closely with the directors and managers at the company and they often expressed how appreciative they were of the work I did for them.

I had started out working full-time for the company, but after about a year of that, we came to the agreement that I would work in the office for only three days per week. This meant that I would be earning less money from this source, but it freed up a lot of time for me to pursue other types of freelance work.

My position as a consultant was by no means guaranteed at any point—I was an expense and had to be constantly proving my worth to the company. It always made me nervous when I would come to the sections in the reports I was working on that called for reducing or eliminating all consultants. And I was eliminated a couple of times, but they always called me back. But the final blow came when a new vice president of the company came on board and decided to move the headquarters to Cincinnati, Ohio.

While some of the people I worked with were relocating, most of my contacts at the company were looking for other jobs. I offered to typeset resumes at no charge for anyone who needed the service, and many people took me up on the offer.

One of the highlight of my time at the company came when a senior vice president came up to me in the hallway and told me that "I did the work of two men." He was an older gentleman and meant no disrespect in comparing me to men. I took this as high praise and was very happy to be recognized for my efforts.

My work with the company came to an end when they completed the move to Ohio. I immediately began sending out letters and resumes to any company whose contact information I could find. Desktop publishing was a growing field and I had a fairly easy time finding freelance jobs with a variety graphic design firms, banks, and other companies in San Francisco. I had developed some useful skills that made me employable, but I was just at the very beginning of what would prove to be a long and challenging road to true financial stability.

First Steps as a Freelancer

I had offers to work as a freelancer on the premises of some companies, but I decided that I wanted to concentrate on building a freelance business that enabled me to work from home. The many people who worked on the premises of their clients were essentially employees of the companies—but working without receiving any employment benefits. Freelancers generally made more per hour in wages than regular employees, but in the end, I think the employees made out better than most freelancers, particularly those who worked on-site but without the benefits of being a full-time employee.

In some ways, I envied the stability that on-site freelancers had in being able to bill a single client for regular work, but they weren't building businesses that would last beyond losing a single client. For me, long-term success has always meant having multiple clients so that my business could survive losing any single one of them.

If I had a business strategy, it was to pursue the type of work that I enjoyed, while trying to keep increasing my income. This turned out to be a pretty good idea as I found myself doing work that I enjoyed and was learning new skills and becoming more of a graphic designer than a production person.

Hanging Out at the Caffe Trieste in North Beach

I had a lot of free time on my hands while I was trying to build my freelance business, especially in the early days and even sometimes after I was relatively established. I don't remember working too many full forty-hour work weeks for the first ten years of my freelance career. This wasn't at all by choice and was a constant source of frustration for me. I wanted—and needed—to work as much as possible, doing everything I could think of to bring in new customers. It just took time to build up my business—seeing many clients come and go for various reasons—but I almost always had enough work to get by fairly well.

Because I was living in San Francisco, finding things to do with my free time was usually not too difficult. I found much of my social life centering around the Caffe Trieste in San Francisco's North Beach district. The Trieste was famous for being a meeting place for the 1950s Beat poets and writers. Some were still hanging around, but most of them were long gone by the time I arrived in the late 1980s.

However, there were still enough old-timers and ambitious new writers and artists at the Caffe Trieste to completely turn my young mind, and I soon found myself having adopting the "artist" ethic of the city. Where I grew up in Michigan the main emphasis seemed to have been on earning a good living—not so much on whether you loved the work, but more on how much you made.

I was a young woman when I first set foot in the Caffe Trieste. I was overwhelmed by the warm greeting that met me from what seemed like dozens of men and women of every description, type, and age. I soon realized that some of these people spent half of their lives at the Caffe Trieste, drinking strong coffee and chatting away with whoever happened to be sitting next to them.

The people at the Caffe Trieste were interested in the fact that I was a freelancer working for book publishers and authors. Some of them were probably hoping that I could somehow help them to get their writing published.

I enjoyed chatting with all kinds of artists, including Joe Rosenthal, the man who took the famous photograph of the raising of the flag on Iwo Jima, which has also been immortalized in statue. Joe was in his 80s when I met him. He was a great guy and I was just happy to be able to sit with him and listen to anything he had to say.

I never spoke to any of them, but famed and acclaimed writers and poets such as Allan Ginsberg, Lawrence Ferlinghetti, and William S. Burroughs were often in the North Beach neighborhood where the Caffe Trieste was located. Lawrence Ferlinghetti was the long-time owner of City Lights Bookstore, located just two blocks from the Caffe Trieste. City Lights was the center of the literary universe for many writers and artists in the area and around the world.

I sent several letters and emails to just about everyone working at City Lights Publishing—including Ferlinghetti himself—but I never received any type of response from any of them. They likely had relationships with their own designers and typesetters, and like most book publishers, were approached by a lot of freelancers. These factors made it a real challenge for a new freelancer to break through.

Socializing at the Caffe Trieste helped to take my mind off some of the anxiety I experienced when worrying what the next day/week/month/year might hold for my always fluctuating income. It was also as inspiring for me to be around people who were succeeding as writers and artists, as it was instructive for me to see the struggles of the many who were failing.

CHAPTER 2

WORKING AS A FREELANCE BOOK TYPESETTER

A stroke of good fortune led me to the Berkeley Macintosh Users Group (BMUG), which had offices in Berkeley, California, a thirty-minute drive from where I lived in San Francisco. BMUG was a well-known and "powerful" Macintosh users group at the time, which meant that they had industry connections and that a lot of people listened to their technical advice and thoughts on Macintosh computers and their many uses.

I looked forward to going to their monthly meetings, which always attracted a fairly large crowd of computer enthusiasts and also many freelancers in various fields. I learned more about computers from BMUG than I ever would have on my own, and engaged with many interesting and talented people at the meetings.

Most of the people I met through BMUG were computer programmers and database experts, although there were some people who were working in the book publishing industry. I never had the interest or ability to understand much about how the computers actually operated, but I learned a lot about how to use computers from spending time with the BMUG folks. This has enabled me to solve on my own almost all of my computer problems and issues that have arisen over the years. I also know when to reach out for help.

Fortunately for me and my fellow computer users, the Macintosh computer operates much the same way that it did when it was first introduced. Because Apple has kept so many things about the way the computer operates the same over so many years, I've been able to keep building on what I know, and to develop a high level of expertise on the Macintosh.

One of the highlights of my BMUG experience was when Steve Jobs presented his NeXT computer to the group in a packed University of California, Berkeley auditorium. But the most important thing to happen to me because of my connection to BMUG was when I read a job posting for a desktop publishing freelancer wanted by a major book publisher located nearby in Menlo Park, California.

Freelancing for a Major Book Publishing Company

As I was making my way to the book publisher's receptionist at the front desk, I saw a fellow desktop publishing freelancer and good friend whom I knew from BMUG passing in the hallway, on his interview with the book production department people. My friend looked much more professional than I did in my more casual work-at-home attire, carrying his leather briefcase and dressed in a great-looking business suit, but it turned out that I ended up getting the freelance job.

The project was a series of standardized tests for schoolchildren grades 5–12. I was too inexperienced to realize that I should have been at least a little concerned when they told me they were having trouble with the project and that it was taking longer to complete than they had anticipated.

I managed to do a good enough job for them to start sending me other books for typesetting on a regular basis. Each new book project seemed to be harder than the last one. I didn't realize at the time that as books go, the textbook designs I was working on were much more difficult and labor intensive than most other types of books. The eye-catching and often elaborate designs were meant to help students to focus on the material. The textbooks also had to go through numerous rounds of revisions before they could be finalized and printed.

I ended up working for many years for a division of the publisher that was located in offices not far from the main company building. This division specialized in publishing books designed for students who learned in "non-traditional" ways, and included more graphics and visual elements than most of the books that I would work on later in my career.

I find that putting together a book is a lot like doing a jigsaw puzzle, which happened to be one of my favorite things to do as a young person. Each of these tasks requires sitting for a prolonged period of time, focusing on minute details, and staying at it until the project is completed.

Unlike putting together a jigsaw puzzle, things don't always fit together perfectly on the pages of a book. Sometimes there can be too much or too little text, or images in sizes or proportions that don't quite work for the page. Typesetting and book layout requires making a series of decisions and adjustments that result in laying out the pages in the most precise and consistent manner possible.

My First Book Production Award

I was absolutely thrilled and very excited upon discovering that I had won a BookBuilders West Book Production Award for a series of textbooks about recycling that I worked on for one of my book publisher clients. My parents were even more thrilled, and it was a welcome reward and validation for all of my hard work.

Having had no formal education in the field of graphic design, I had felt like an outsider in my own industry for many years. My initial opportunities to work with book publishers, left me very impressed by the skills of the book designers. As time went by, I developed the skills and the desire to become a book designer myself. I had the opportunity to learn from a variety of these folks, and I ultimately figured out what they were doing and how they did it.

After a lot of trial and error and many years of practice, there came a point where I actually did know what I was doing as a book designer. I have a fairly eclectic style, but if you studied the body of my work, you would see that I tend to make certain design choices that prioritize readability and clarity over all things. Everything that I put on a page must be there for a reason. If it doesn't serve a purpose, such as directing the reader's eye to a certain point, a design element must look really great to justify its placement in a book.

Typesetting vs. Page Layout or Formatting

When I first started out I was a "desktop publisher," but I soon became a "book typesetter," and sometimes publishers called me a "book formatter." Like the term "desktop publishing," which was just another way of saying "graphic design on a computer," a lot of different job titles are used to describe the same thing. A well-meaning manager at one big corporation used to call me "Apple Annie," a nickname that never sat well with me, but that I took in the complimentary spirit that was intended.

I prefer to call myself a book typesetter as do most of my more established book publisher clients, who send me purchase orders for "typesetting" work. The only other term I like to use to describe my work is "page layout," and I've often been called a "layout artist," which acknowledges that book production is more than just typesetting the text in the correct fonts. Laying out the text and images on the page in the most attractive and appealing way possible requires a lot of artistry and creativity.

I was once called old-fashioned and out-of-step by a prospective book publisher client because I used the word "typesetting" in one of the introductory emails I sent to him. I went for an interview at his home office in the Los Angeles area and saw that most of the people there were young, maybe just out of college. I agree that typesetting is an old-fashioned term, but the only other equivalent would be book composition, another common book production term that isn't used much today.

CHAPTER 3

EVERYTHING KEEPS CHANGING

When my children's textbook publisher client announced that they were moving their headquarters from California to New York, it lit a real fire under me to find new clients, and ended up marking the end of my relationship with the company. Most of my contacts left their jobs with the book publisher and stayed behind in California, but some of the more senior people ended up moving to New York.

I never heard from any of the people I worked with again, but a few years later I was contacted by an editor who had worked for the publisher and was now starting his own book production company. He was looking for a freelance book designer and typesetter to work with. We ended up collaborating on many book projects, including two best-selling series of computer instruction books for a major U.S. book publisher.

Finding BookBuilders West

Aside from the connections I made at the Berkeley Macintosh Users Group, discovering and then becoming a member of BookBuilders West, a local book publishing industry group, turned out to be just about the best thing that I've ever done to build my freelance business.

The main reason I joined the group was to have access to their member directory, where I hoped to find the names and contact information of publishing professionals who might be interested in sending me freelance work. I also started attending the BookBuilders West monthly meetings that the group held at the Fort Mason Officer's Club, which wasn't far from where I lived in San Francisco's Marina District.

I always felt like a fish out of water at these meetings, but I forced myself to keep attending. It seemed that everyone in the room already knew one another, and for the most part they did. Most of the people at the meetings worked at book publishing companies or book printers and a lot of them had been working together for many years.

I did my best to mingle and interact with the other book publishing professionals, but this type of socializing was never my strong point. I've always been more comfortable and better at reaching out to people I don't know through telephone or email.

The one person that I did know and always saw at the meetings told me that she didn't want to talk to me because she was trying to meet new people and make new connections. I did much better at the sit-down dinner part of the evening, which came after a long hour of socializing and networking in the lounge area of the Fort Mason Officer's Club.

There were about eight people at each table and the conversation usually flowed pretty easily. I don't think I ever made any direct contacts with new clients at the meetings, but I learned a lot about many factors affecting the book publishing industry, and benefited from listening to the guest speakers on topics that went beyond my usual focus on book design and typesetting.

I was very excited when I finally received my printed copy of the BookBuilders West member directory, which would be the first of many to come over the years. The directory contained the contact information for hundreds of San Francisco Bay Area publishing professionals, complete with their titles and mailing addresses.

I loaded up on Crane's off-white resume paper and envelopes and sent out my cover letter, resume, and samples to everyone in the directory that I thought might possibly be interested in using my services.

Good timing was on my side and I received many positive responses from my first mailing. I got real paying freelance jobs from some publishers and promises of future work from others. And I needed the work after having just lost my book publisher client who had made up a major portion of my income for many years.

Although I had some expectations that I would hear from some of the people I had worked with at the book publisher when they were settled in their new jobs, it never happened. But the book publisher's name still looked great on my resume, and just having worked for the well-known publisher helped me to find new freelance work. I owed them a lot for teaching me most of what I knew about book design and typesetting to that point.

Freelancing for Another Major Book Publisher

I was very eager to work as a freelancer for a well-known and well-respected book publisher located in San Francisco, whose contact information was listed in the Book-Builders West member directory. I sent my promotional letters to at least a dozen people at the company before I was finally called in for an interview.

They were in the process of converting all of their book production from the traditional book typesetters they had been using for many years to the new the Macintosh desktop publishing systems. They were looking for freelancers for what they called "bread-and-butter" typesetting work. This sounded great to me, and I was thrilled when they started scheduling me for projects on a regular basis, and ultimately becoming a steady source of income for me for many years.

I loved working for this book publisher and became friendly with many of the book production editors that I worked with on projects. I had a lot of respect and admiration for the accomplished book editors, who knew everything about language and editing that I was lacking. After years of working on books, I've absorbed a lot of lessons about good writing, editing, and correct punctuation, but I've never had the formal training or mentoring that is usually required to become a great editor.

The editors managed books through the various stages of production, working with me on the typesetting and layout (I wasn't working as a book designer at this point), but also hiring illustrators, proofreaders, indexers, and anyone else needed to produce the book. I wasn't involved at all with any work on the book covers, but I admired the work of the cover designers.

They were always coming up with a seemingly endless array of new ideas for great covers. How the cover designers came up with their ideas was still a big mystery to me. I loved looking at and studying the work of good and great cover designers, but didn't think I would ever have the skills to be a book cover designer myself.

However, I had thought that I already knew everything there was to know about book typesetting and layout, but soon figured out that I had a lot to learn about the finer points of typesetting from the editors and production people at my new book publisher client. The editors were patient with my mistakes and oversights and told me that I made fewer errors than most of their other typesetters.

I was also beginning to understand a lot more about how book designers did their creative and technical work. With time and experience, I began to develop a sense of what worked well with book designs—and what didn't work as well—and began the process of coming up with my own design style.

The book designs that I was working with were becoming increasingly sophisticated and elaborate as the computer layout programs offered new and advanced features that enabled more complex designs and layouts.

The Macintosh computers had become so much faster than in the early days of desktop publishing, and imagination and ability seemed to be the only limitations to what could be done.

A lot of books are typeset using design templates that publishers develop using in-house and freelance designers. When I first started freelancing with this San Francisco publisher, they had about a dozen design templates that they used for most of the books they produced. Each template had different fonts and graphic elements, but were generic enough that they could be used effectively for books on a variety of topics.

The book production managers and editors would try to choose the most appropriate design from among the templates, but some special or important books got their own custom designs. I always enjoyed seeing what the book designers would come up with, and did my best to perfectly execute their designs to their often very detailed specifications. Sometimes I was asked to modify or enhance an existing template, but I was considered to be a typesetter, and was never asked to develop any new templates or to work on any custom interior book designs.

I worked as a freelance typesetter for many great projects for over ten years and was very surprised and disappointed when I was informed that they would no longer be working with any U.S. typesetters. The major

U.K. publisher that had purchased my book publisher client a few years earlier had decided to outsource all of their typesetting work to book production companies in India.

As it turned out, they didn't send all of their books for typesetting overseas right away, but they did outsource most of them. I continued to work for them for a few years as one of a handful U.S. typesetters still working as freelancers for the company, but they ultimately stopped working with all U.S. typesetters in favor of outsourcing all of the work to India.

After going through the experience of losing two big clients as a major source of freelance work, I was determined that I would never be so dependent on any one client again, knowing that they could leave me at any time. The hunt was on for a new batch of clients.

Freelancing for a Prestigious University Press

One of my book publisher colleagues did me the big favor of passing my contact information along to the managing editor of a prestigious university press that was located in New York. I was impressed and thrilled at the prospect of working for this well-respected university press. I was always excited to find a new client and usually called my now-cheerleading parents almost every time I found a new client or received a new book to work on.

The first couple of books went well and the production people said nice things to me about my excellent work. The third book had a number of very detailed graphs. The plotting points were not included, which would have made it much easier for me to render the graphs. As it turned out, the method I chose for recreating a couple of the drawings resulted in some of the graph points being in the wrong position.

It was unusual for me to be working on graphs at all. In my previous experience as a freelancer for book publishers, anything that could be considered "art"—drawings, charts, or figures—was sent to a freelancer illustrator who would supply files for all of the artwork in the book. The illustrators could produce more accurate and better-looking artwork than I could as a book typesetter. It's a completely different skill set, and it goes both ways: most illustrators would have a hard time typesetting a book.

I've worked on my share of simple illustrations and figures, but I usually found that I earned less money doing that type of work than I did working as a freelance typesetter. I always try to lead with my strengths, and I was more skilled as a typesetter, where I could leverage my speed, efficiency, and accuracy to increase my productivity and thereby earn more money.

I fixed the graphs for the book and thought nothing of it. However, an angry editor sent a nasty note to her manager about the graphs, raging about my incompetence. It turned out to be the last book that I ever received from them. My apologetic production manager contact told me that they had decided to work exclusively with larger typesetting firms.

Unfortunately, she also decided to show me the unkind letter written to her by the editor about the errors I made in the graphs. She told me she was showing me the letter so I could see the kind of difficult people she had to work with, but I would have preferred to have been spared the vitriol.

After working with them for a couple of months, I had already grown out of being star-struck by the name and reputation of the university press. The work had been very challenging and I had agreed to work for too little pay because I wanted to be associated with the university. On the bright side, this was the last time I was overly impressed by the reputation of a publisher or author—although I never fail to show respect to each and every one of my clients.

When I was first starting out, I could hardly believe that anyone would be willing to pay me to do the work that I loved so much, let alone major book publishers. As I became more confident in my skills and ability to attract new customers, it became easier to let go of the hurt feelings associated with projects that ended badly.

Freelancing for a Medium-Sized Book Publisher

I found the contact information for my next client, a medium-sized publisher in Palo Alto, California, through the BookBuilders West member directory. I had been sending their director of publications my mailings for at least two years, when she responded with a note saying that she didn't have any work for me right now, but that I should keep sending her my materials. I appreciated her taking the time to write this encouraging letter, and kept sending my mailings until I was eventually rewarded with a big freelance typesetting project.

The new project was an instructional manual with one volume for participants and another volume for the facilitator. The company owned the rights to a very popular psychological profiling test, and all of their books had something to do with the topic. The instruction manuals were used in training sessions and included a large section of images of the many slides that were used during the presentations.

Although they never hired me for design work, I learned a lot about good design practices from working with the files of the highly regarded book designer that they used for most of their projects. I was still somewhat in awe of how designers came up with the ideas for their layouts. This designer used a lot of stylized patterns and shapes as background elements and to highlight elements in the books and manuals.

One of the many things that I appreciated about my many years of working with this publisher was their excellent copyeditor, who had the best and neatest handwriting that I've ever seen. I've worked with hundreds of editors and proofreaders, and fortunately most of them have fairly good and readable handwriting. Editors can ask me to make hundreds or even thousands of text corrections to a book after it's been completely typeset, so it really helps if I'm able to easily understand the editor's comments.

Working with revisions got a lot easier once editors were able to mark text and formatting changes by adding comments on the PDF file. Before PDF was introduced, I received most book revisions as printed pages with handwritten comments and maybe a Microsoft Word file of longer text inserts. It's much easier for me to make changes using a marked-up PDF where I can cut and paste the new text, rather than typing in any new text as before—with the possibility of my introducing new typos into the book.

I was very happy working as a typesetting freelancer for the psychology publisher for over twenty years until my main contact at the company retired from her long-time job, and I never heard from the publisher again. Once again, I was highly motivated to seek out new clients, and returned to sending out my cover letters, resumes, and design samples to hundreds of potential new customers. Losing this long-time source of steady freelance work was a big blow to me, but I soon recovered and had new work flowing in.

Failing to Succeed

As much as I tried to do my best work for clients—that I was capable of at the time—I ran into at least my fair share of the inevitable client break-ups that come with being a freelancer (or any type of business or employee). Fortunately, each failure or loss motivated me to seek out the next opportunity. Nothing inspires me more to go looking for new clients as much as losing an existing client.

Reaching out to new clients always gave me something productive to do, even if I was just biding my time waiting for the next author or publisher client to ask me to work on their new book. And I found that just going through the motions of seeking out new work was more than just therapeutic for me—it inevitably led to my finding new clients.

In the early days of my book publishing freelancer career, I wasn't even sure if I wanted to be an editor, proofreader, typesetter, or book designer. But I always tried to go where my strengths led me, trying to figure out how best to utilize my skills and opportunities. I received enough praise and positive feedback from my publisher and author clients that I knew I was a good typesetter.

I rarely typed more than a few sentences at a time—authors and publishers almost always provide Microsoft Word files of any text for the book. But my speedy and accurate typing skills and ability to maneuver quickly on the computer keyboard helped me to work much faster than other typesetters who were doing similar work. This meant that I was earning more money than most of my colleagues, and gave me the confidence to continue pursuing freelance work on a full-time basis.

Because I usually charge customers by the page or project for my work, I've been able to earn more money if I can complete the work in less time—without making errors that would cause me to lose the client. Being rewarded for my speed and accuracy was a huge motivator for me to keep finding ways to increase my productivity, while always improving the quality of my work.

Finding a Design Mentor

I had the very good fortune of meeting a very creative and skilled graphic designer and illustrator when I attended a computer graphic design workshop that he was teaching at the *San Francisco Examiner* in downtown San Francisco. In addition to working as a staff illustrator for the *Examiner,* he was always busy with freelance projects and creating his own works of fine art; elaborate and colorful illustrations that used the latest features in Adobe Illustrator and Photoshop. I admired everything about his work, particularly his use of color in the innovative, intricate, and beautiful compositions.

I was still very much in awe of the book designers I was working with. I loved everything about my typesetting work, but I was fascinated by how designers came up with the ideas for their layouts. As a typesetter, I was given a design template that had been created by a book designer to be used to typeset and lay out the book pages. The designers used various fonts and design elements (images, colors, shapes, and lines, for example) to create a more or less unique identity for each book.

My new graphic designer/artist friend and mentor was the first design professional to ever encourage me to become a designer in my own right. He asked me why I was content to be just a typesetter, when it was so much more fun and satisfying to work as a designer.

When I was first getting started in the late 1980s and early 1990s it was more than enough that you knew how to use a Macintosh computer to find work as a typesetting or book production freelancer—or even as a full-time employee. The desktop publishing industry continued to evolve, and by the mid-1990s, trained graphic designers with college degrees had replaced many of the people who had gotten work on the basis of their Macintosh skills, but lacked the design and artistic training and ability of this new generation of design professionals.

I was an English major in college and never went to art school or had any formal graphic design training, or even much computer training. I'm very much self-taught, having learned almost everything I know on my own, mostly from problem-solving on projects that people were paying me to work on. At times, my lack of formal training made me hesitant to pursue certain challenging types of work with new or existing clients. I feared that I might make mistakes due to my lack of knowledge and experience that could cost my customers time and money—and cause me to lose the client in the process.

Fortunately, the range of projects I was working on kept expanding and I was working on a lot challenging book projects. I had no choice but to seize the opportunities as they arose, and to keep expanding well beyond my comfort zone. I did my best to increase and refine my book design and production skills wherever possible, but not at the expense of a client. If a project came to me that was too far beyond my abilities, or if I thought that someone else would do a better job for the client, I would turn down the job, and possibly save myself and the client a lot of trouble.

Figuring Out that I'm Not an Editor

I spent hours reading every day as a young person, but never studied or understood the finer points of English grammar enough to be a great book editor. I learned very little about how to work for a book publisher as an editor when I was an English major at the University of Michigan. Because I always got good grades on my English papers, I fancied myself to be a good writer, which would naturally lead to my being a good editor and proofreader.

One of the downsides of my lifetime career as a freelancer is that I never went through the in-house training or mentoring that teaches new editors (or designers) what they need to know to do be great at their jobs. I might actually have learned to be a great book editor if I had ever been properly trained, but that never happened. I was hired to work as an editor and proofreader for some book projects early in my career, but I never had the type of patience required for the work, or the expertise needed to do a great job. I know most of what's required for great editing, but my skills don't compare to those of the many wonderful editors that I've worked with.

Having confidence in my ability as a skilled typesetter and then designer has been essential to my efforts to seek out and retain new author and publisher customers. If I had tried to build up my skills and client base as an editor, I think my career path would have been much the same, but without as much volatility and the constant need to seek out new work. Editors charge a lot more than I do for the work they do for authors—in total, if not by the hour. I rarely spend more than a few weeks working on a book project, whereas editors can spend months or even years working on an author's manuscript.

Finding work as a freelance editor or proofreader seemed to be a lot easier than finding freelance book design and typesetting work. Book publishers are almost always looking for new freelance editors and proofreaders. Because editors and proofreaders spent so much more time working on their projects than I did as the designer and typesetter, I had to find a lot more books to work on than the editors and proofreaders did to keep myself fully employed.

However, book designers and typesetters can earn a lot more money than editors, which has always been a big motivator for me. Also, I always ended up with a lot of free time almost every day after finishing all of my work, whereas many of the editors I know are working night and day to keep up with their deadlines.

Leveraging the Latest Technology to Increase My Productivity

Being able to leverage the ever-increasing speed of the Macintosh computers and software to increase my productivity was a major factor in helping me to build a profitable freelance book typesetting business. The editors and proofreaders, who were already being paid less per hour than I was able to charge still had to read every word on every page and attend to the many details that go into properly editing a book. The computer enabled searching and replacing of text, but editors and proofreaders still had to take the time to read (and re-read) everything, and couldn't take advantage of the increasing speed and abilities of computers as much as I could as a typesetter.

The layout programs kept getting better—starting with Aldus PageMaker; moving on to Quark XPress; and then the now-current standard, Adobe InDesign.

New features in the programs enabled me to automate a lot of the work that had previously been quite time consuming. I was able to produce more pages in less time than before while my page rate stayed the same, which meant that I was able to earn more money with less effort.

CHAPTER 4

BECOMING A FREELANCE BOOK TYPESETTER

loved typesetting books and always found something to enjoy about almost every project that I worked on. Some were great because I could get them done very quickly—often in a day or two when the publisher gave me two weeks to complete the book. I would have made much less money if I had been charging by the hour for my work. But since the billing was by the page, I was rewarded for being able to do the work quickly. I always enjoy the challenge of working on difficult projects, even though I usually made more money per hour on the easier projects.

When I first graduated from college I saw myself as a potential writer and editor, and had no thoughts whatsoever of working in the graphic design field. However, I would soon learn that I already had many of the skills needed to be a typesetter. Learning and practicing the craft always seemed to come very easily and naturally to me.

I chose to focus on typesetting and laying out book pages because it happened that I was very good at doing this type of work. I really enjoyed the process of working on the Macintosh computer to lay out pages. And I was well paid for my efforts, making more money than most of my colleagues due to my speed and ability to take on a lot of diverse and varied projects.

When I first started typesetting books, the instructions for the book design came to me in the form of five to ten pages of written design and type specifications—with no visual samples at all. I learned how to transform the designers' detailed directions and layout specifications into actual typeset book pages. My publisher clients were almost always very satisfied with the quality of my work.

I was happy typesetting books using other people's designs for many years until I built up the confidence to start designing books on my own. One of the great things about studying graphic design and typography is that there are examples everywhere you look. I began observing and studying the design of books, magazines, newspapers, streets signs, and advertisements in an attempt to make myself into a real designer and not just a typesetter.

As much as I loved working as a typesetter, there was more prestige in being a designer. But as it turned out, I always earned more money as a typesetter than as a designer. I was able to charge anywhere from $300 to $1,000 for most book designs, but the average invoice for typesetting was usually higher than that. However, I was able to attract a lot freelance work because I was now offering both book design and typesetting services.

It's easier for a publisher to work with one freelancer on the design and typesetting of a book than to hire two people to work on the project. Designing books definitely added to my income, but more importantly, book publishers were increasingly interested in working with me on projects because I could now provide both design and typesetting services.

Working as a Freelance Book Designer

I was developing to the point where I felt I was at least as good of a book design as most of the other designers that I worked with. I continued to learn and draw inspiration from working with other book designers, and hoped that my designs might one day inspire others. I was very pleased and a little nervous when I started getting my first book design assignments after adding "book designer" when I sent out my emails reaching out to new customers.

I think that some of my early designs were decent, or at least pretty good, but I continued to evolve and develop my design skills and style. After a while, I even felt confident enough to take some chances with my designs. And it turned out that a lot of authors and publishers often chose what I considered to be the most unusual or non-traditional design samples that I sent them.

When I first started designing books I would come up with dozens of possible designs with different fonts, layouts, and design elements. I would pick my favorite three or four designs and then submit the PDF samples to the client. As time went on and I become a better and more efficient book designer, I didn't need to come up with as many designs to get to a few good ones. I began to focus on creating three or four designs to present as samples to choose from or modify as needed.

Sometimes a client doesn't like any of my designs and asks me to send completely new samples, but most authors and publishers choose from one of my samples, requesting little or no modifications. I'm always happy to make changes to any of my book designs as this often leads to the best-looking books.

Getting the Book Design Sample Approved

The design samples are sent out to the various people involved in the project, including the author, editor, and art director, who decide together if any of the designs will work for the book. I expect the client to request some modifications to my designs after the initial presentation of the samples.

Some of the best designs can come from a productive collaboration between the designer, editor, and author. However, having too many people giving their opinions on a design can sometimes be a bad thing, and end up compromising the quality and effectiveness of a design. I always hope that the client picks my favorite design for the book, but I always defer to the choices and preferences of my clients, who know the book topic and potential audience better than I do.

My role and purpose is to give the client at least what they're looking for, and hopefully enhance the book in some ways that they weren't even expecting. As much as typesetting is all about speed and accuracy, I think good graphic design is about slowing down to give the ideas room to flow as freely as possible. I tried to give myself the time needed to slow down and relax, which often led to my most attractive and effective designs.

What Makes a Great Book Design?

Just about anything that can be printed on a piece of paper can work as a design element for a book. I have many hundreds of different fonts on my computers, including dozens of dingbat (printer ornament) fonts, which have all kinds of icons, pictures, and geometric shapes that can be used as design elements.

There are online sites like istockphoto.com and stock.adobe.com (Adobe Stock Images) that sell downloadable electronic files of photographs and illustrations that can be used for designs of any type. I think some of the best designs use a combination of photographs and graphic elements such as floral or geometric ornaments. But you can take any simple form or shape and turn it into an interesting and attractive design.

I've typeset—and read—many books where the designers were just decorating the pages, using graphic elements in ways that added very little to the readability of the page. I think it's important to create a coherent book design that adds something to the reader's experience—making it easier to read and absorb information, where everything on the page works to keep the reader's attention.

When I was working on a new book design, a senior editor at the book publisher told me that she should to be able to tell the hierarchy of the different levels of subheads just by looking at any one of the subheads—without reference to the size or boldness of the other subheads. I was grateful for the great advice and it changed my way of designing books. As a primarily self-taught book designer, this basic book design principle had never occurred to me.

When I submit design samples to clients I always do my best to create something special, unique, and aesthetically pleasing. It's not easy to define what that special quality consists of, but there's something satisfying about looking at a book or page design that works as a whole.

All Email, No More Phone Calls

In the early days of my freelance work, I used to enjoy long conversations on the telephone or in person with my book publisher clients. But by the mid-1990s, most of my clients were contacting me exclusively through email.

At first I found it all very strange and off-putting that clients were hiring, and on occasion, firing me, all by email, but the telephone was considered impersonal compared to face-to-face contact when it first came into use. I did my best to be friendly and cheerful in my emails to customers, starting with a friendly "Hi" and ending with "Best wishes and thanks!" or some other upbeat message.

Soon enough, I completely adapted to the world of all email communication and no phone calls, and came to prefer typing out my thoughts rather than speaking them out loud. This fundamentally changed the nature of my communications with clients. In the past, customers would call me to schedule me for a new job and then it wasn't unusual to stay on the phone for a prolonged chat. Despite the risk of revealing more to clients about my personal life than might be beneficial, it led to a better sense of friendship and appreciation for one another. And maybe made it more likely for them to keep me around as a freelancer rather than moving on to someone else.

I'm always very careful to double check and proofread all of the business emails I send out. I'm usually writing to very literate editors and book publishing people, and I don't want to make mistakes that diminish their confidence in my skills. I remain in business because my clients trust in my abilities and accuracy, and I don't want to give them any reason to think otherwise.

As it's our main way of communicating, I view each email I send or receive as an opportunity to build on my relationship with a client. I always try to include a "Thank you!" or "Happy day to you!" in my emails. I want clients to enjoy and value working with me and for all of us to look forward to working on our next project together.

Always Waiting on the Next Project

I always ended up with a lot of free time between book jobs—not by choice, that's just how it worked out. I was often frustrated at not being able to work as much as I wanted to, but I tried to make the most out of my time. And San Francisco was an easy place to find something to do or someone to talk to.

I think the main factor that kept me in business for so many years was that I always started reaching out to new customers when I had more than two or three days in a row without any work coming in. Taking this action helped to calm my anxiety about my always fluctuating income, and did a lot to build my freelance business by attracting new customers.

Should I Hire Other Freelancers to Work for Me?

When I was a few years into my freelance business and still focusing mostly on typesetting, I considered trying to build a business with other freelancers working for me. I decided against pursuing this route because I had seen other businesses of this type succeed for a while and then ultimately fail. I was afraid that if I ended up just managing other freelancers, I would fail to develop and maintain the computer and design skills that I would need to survive as a freelancer for the long term.

My decision to develop my own skills rather than hiring other freelancers to do the work for me turned out to be a smart move, especially when book publishers began outsourcing most of their book production work to India. It had been hard enough to generate enough business to keep myself busy. It's unlikely that I could have managed to keep a larger operation in business with so much of the work going overseas. And I saw that many book production services companies failed at this point, including some of my own clients.

Trying to Freelance for the U.S. Government

I decided to try reaching out to potential U.S. government and related book publishers because so many book publishers were now outsourcing their work to India—one major book publisher client told me that they were no longer "allowed" by upper management to work with U.S. designers or typesetters.

I spent many weeks and months looking online for the names and email addresses of government publishing departments and employees. It was easy enough to find a general contact email address, but locating the names and email addresses of the art director, production manager, managing editor, or whoever was in charge of hiring freelancers was a time-consuming and often frustrating process.

I got a lot more nos than yeses and a couple of "please take me off your mailing list." One person I sent my email to accused me of sending out a mass mailing. I'm not exactly sure what qualifies as a "mass" mailing and why that would be such a bad thing. But I wasn't stopped from pursuing my goals by the negative feedback—it was annoying and sometimes demoralizing, but it also motivated me to pursue other clients.

It took a lot of self-confidence, sheer staying power, and sometimes just bravado for me to keep at it year after year. But my process of contacting publishers through email was a time-tested and proven method for getting new freelance work. I won't say that I wasn't discouraged at times, but then I usually would receive a new project to work on or a kind response that helped me to press on.

Freelancing for a Prestigious U.S. Government Press

One of my cover letter, resume, and samples emails ended up at a well-respected U.S. government press located in Washington, DC. My timing was right this time, and it turned out that they were actually looking for a freelance typesetter to work on their books. There would be no design work involved, just what turned out to be the fairly complicated typesetting of books with lots of figures and tables and sometimes mathematical equations, which required special attention to be properly typeset.

I was thrilled to be working with the great editors and staff, and all of my contacts also seemed to love working for the prestigious publisher. I felt as though it was an honor to be working on these books, and I still feel that way after over twenty years and hundreds of books.

I thought I was a great typesetter when I began working on books for this publisher. But once again, it turned out that I had much to learn, not only about the finer points of book typesetting and layout, but also better ways of using Adobe InDesign, the main computer program I used for almost all of my work.

I'd been considered an "expert" in InDesign for many years, but the people working for this publisher taught me new and better ways of using the program. Upgrading my skills so that I can do better design and typesetting work for my clients is the best way I know to keep them coming back to me with more projects.

Freelancing for a Large Independent Publisher

I expanded my hunt for U.S. government publishers to any book publishers in the Washington, D.C. area. One of my best freelance opportunities—and one of my favorite clients of all time—came as a result of my email campaign, which arrived at the right place at the right time.

I don't know if the production staff were actively looking for new book design and typesetting freelancers to expand their book production capacity, but they began sending me projects right away. The first book I designed and typeset for my new book publisher client was about the disappearance and possible fate of Amelia Earhart, who disappeared on her solo flight over the Atlantic Ocean in 1937. I used a photograph of Earhart standing by the airplane before the flight as a design element on the chapter openers.

The next project I worked on was a big book about Judy Garland, which covered her entire career and had dozens of photographs of Garland and her many performances. I found a great illustration of old-fashioned theater curtains that I placed on all of the chapter opener pages—with the chapter title and introductory text falling within the area between the half-opened curtains. Fortunately, the production people at the publisher loved my design samples, which was the start of a decades-long freelance relationship that I will always value and treasure.

In the beginning, the publisher kept me busy designing and typesetting all kinds of books, but over time they developed the capacity to typeset a lot of their books using an in-house system. I worried that this development might be the end of my freelance work from the publisher, but they kept sending me new projects to work on. But they stopped sending me the simpler, mostly-text books, and began sending me some of the most challenging projects of my career.

I enjoyed the challenge of working on many long and difficult U.S. government publications. Many of the books were made up of a series of tables and graphs and very little text. Some of the books had only three or four tables in total, but they went on for hundreds of pages. A lot of focus and deep concentration is needed to accurately typeset and lay out long or complicated tables to the exact design and type specifications and requirements. I always tried to figure out the best ways to approach the difficult projects and managed to beat every deadline.

I typeset many editions of an annual book that the publisher produced for the Gallup opinion polls. There were over 1,500 charts and graphs in the five-hundred page books, which turned out to be some of the hardest and most demanding projects I've ever worked on—and the new editions of the book kept coming back to me year after year.

When I first started on the project I was given three months to typeset the complete book—in acknowledgment of the difficulty of project. Unless they were trying to rush a book through production, I was usually given two weeks to complete the design and typesetting of most books. The schedule kept getting tighter and tighter for the Gallup book with each new edition, until I was asked to provide proof pages within three weeks. I either had to figure out a better and faster way to lay out the pages, or work day and night to complete the job.

I felt pressured and somewhat overwhelmed by the demands of working on these time-consuming and complicated books. But this also made me highly motivated to find better and more efficient ways of working to make the process go faster without sacrificing quality in any way. I finished the Gallup book in about two weeks to the satisfaction of everyone involved.

Because many of the books I worked on for this book publisher were so difficult and took up so much of my time, I was reluctant to reach out to new customers for fear of getting more work than I could handle. At this time, the freelance work from this one client made up the greater part of my income, but I had three other regular book publishers clients that also kept me fairly busy with freelance work.

I was enjoying more financial stability than I had previously, but it seemed that I was always waiting by the mailbox for the next check to arrive. I probably worried and suffered more than I needed to, but the constant uncertainty as to where my next paycheck would come from—and my always fluctuating income—took a toll on my peace of mind.

Freelancing for the Office of the President of the United States

The longest book I ever worked on was an 1,800-page report for the Office of the United States President. The production editor at my book publisher client was working closely with a secretary at the White House who was in charge of the project.

We were given a copy of the last edition of the report, which judging from the fonts and layout choices, had been done in the early days of desktop publishing using the original Macintosh fonts. The book's production editor and I decided that it would be a great idea to update the design and fonts so that the report would look better and more current and be easier to read. I submitted a few different design samples and after some back and forth, we decided on a new design for the book.

It wasn't a very difficult book to typeset, and I was very happy to be able to charge for 1,800 pages at my standard page rate. The editor and I both thought the new book pages looked great, and were equally dismayed and surprised when the White House secretary said that she actually wanted the new book to look exactly like the old one.

I don't know if this was her decision alone or came from above, but I was grateful that my publisher client agreed to pay me to redo the entire book. I never want it to appear as though I'm taking advantage of a bad situation or benefiting from a client's pain, so I did the work at a much-reduced rate compared to the first round.

Freelancing for Christian Publishers

In my perpetual online quest to find for new book publisher clients, I came across some websites that listed the names and contact information for hundreds of production managers and editors working at large and small U.S. Christian publishers. Good timing was on my side this time, and several of the publishers were receptive to the idea of working with me as a freelancer for the design and typesetting of their books.

I started working as a freelance book designer and typesetter for a publisher of Christian-themed books in Chattanooga, Tennessee, that I found through online membership directory on the Christian Book Publishers website. I worked for over ten years with their wonderful production manager, until his passing after a long battle with cancer. I continued to work for the publisher for a few years after that until all of my colleagues and contacts at the company had moved on to other jobs.

I've worked on books for many other Christian book publishers that I've located through my online searches—and some of them just found their own way to me. Many of these publications have had very high design standards that rivaled the best of the largest and most prestigious book publishers that I've worked for. The books tended to use a lot of engaging graphics and other elements to help maintain the reader's attention.

Freelancing for Children's Books Publishers

I've designed and typeset many hundreds of children's books both for established book publishers and for many self-publishing authors. Most of the children's books are thirty-two pages or less—some can be less than sixteen pages—so my usual method of charging $3.00-$6.00 per page doesn't work in this case. I typically charge in the area of $300.00-$400.00 to design and lay out most children's books, but have worked on some for more and many for less.

Unlike the non-fiction books with lots of text and tables and figures that make up the majority of my work, children's books are usually a lot simpler to work on overall, but require a lot of attention to minute details such as the exact and proper placement of the text and the sizing and cropping of illustrations.

Aside from arranging the illustrations on the page, my main job is to place the text for the book in the perfect spot, usually in an area left by the artist in the illustration with few or no elements in the background that would obscure the text or make it hard to read.

I find that most of the self-publishing authors who come to me for design and typesetting of their children's books are great to work with and appreciative of the services that I provide them. They typically come to me after all of the illustrations for the book have been completed by a freelance illustrator. I've seen all kinds of artwork for children's books over the years. The quality and style of the artwork can range from "just okay" to "great," but I'm always happy to bring my clients' book publishing aspirations to life, and put in my best efforts to make their books the best they can be.

Freelancing for a Small Children's Books Publisher

One of the highlights of my experience working on children's books was typesetting a series of books for young children for a small book publisher located in Massachusetts. I connected with the publisher through one of my cold-call email campaigns that arrived when they were looking for a new freelance typesetter to work with.

I worked closely with the art director to produce the books in the exact and very precise style required by the publisher, and ended up learning some things that I hadn't previously known about working with children's books. I worked on dozens of books in the series over the course of several years, which might have continued on a while longer if my art director contact at the company hadn't moved on to another job.

I didn't make any particular efforts to reach out to the art director's replacement at the company, and the flow of work came to a halt. Looking back, I made a mistake in not reaching out to someone else at the company and at least trying to retain the book publisher as a client.

CHAPTER 5

KEEPING BUSY AS A FREELANCER

I was mostly hard at work designing and typesetting books for a variety of large and small publishers and self-publishing authors. My early Macintosh skills had placed me in a good position to attract new customers for my freelance business. If anything, I had better clients than I really deserved at first. However, I was highly motivated to keep learning and eventually became a pretty good book designer and an even better typesetter.

I don't think I would have even considered starting my own business if I hadn't grown up working at my family's men's clothing store in Detroit, Michigan. The store had several people working as tailors and seamstresses in a walled-off space at the back of the store. From an early age, I saw how they worked to satisfy the customers' needs and even whims, while producing high-quality work—more or less on schedule.

The tailor shop seemed to be perpetually one day behind on their work, but could usually finish things up quickly if a customer came to call early or on-time for their tailored clothing. I remember many times having to apologize to customers and tell them that their clothing wasn't quite ready yet, and offering a cup of coffee or a glass of wine while they waited, or even worse, having to ask them to come back another time.

My experience working at the family business taught me many of the things I would need to know to manage my own business one day. But no lesson was as important as seeing how our expert salespeople interacted with our mostly affluent customers—doing their utmost to please everyone, while maintaining their own personal dignity and space.

Freelancing for the Professor

My connection with a coin collector and retired professor came through a referral from another client who had worked on the author's last book. The new book had hundreds of photographs of rare and ancient bronze coins that had to be precisely arranged on the pages. The professor was a well-known coin collector and a professor of psychology at San Francisco State University and had published many books on different topics. This book was a catalogue of his collection of ancient Greek and Roman bronze coins.

The professor was about eighty years old at the time we worked on the project, and was one of the few clients that I've ever typed a full manuscript for—let alone a book full of Green and Latin inscriptions. Luckily the work was spread out of several months and the professor was very understanding of any time constraints that arose for me.

We met each week at the author's home, which was filled with walls and cases full of rare and ancient artifacts from his collection. I would give him the typeset pages from the last week, and he would give me new sheets of lined yellow legal paper with handwritten descriptions of the coins, including dates and the Greek or Latin inscriptions that appeared on the coins. The descriptions included things like: "Demeter holding a sheaf of wheat."

The text appeared on one side of the two-page book spread. The opposing page had the coins neatly arranged in rows by a freelance graphic artist that the professor hired for the purpose. Unlike me, who did everything on the Macintosh computer, this artist did everything by hand, pasting the photographs of the coins on white boards for the professor to review.

At one point, the artist decided on her own to vary the "dull" and orderly layouts, arranging the coins as though they were parts of a fancy necklace. The professor rejected the pages right away, but I think he kept a few of the necklace coin arrangements in the book, joking that readers would think that he had "lost his mind" during the production of the book.

Freelancing for Another Major U.S. Book Publisher

As a result of another one of my email campaigns, I connected with a production manager at a division of a highly respected U.S. book publisher, who hired me to work as a freelance book designer and typesetter for their textbooks.

I came up with a good idea for the design of my first book project, and at first they seemed to be very happy with my work. The editor told me she really liked the preliminary design samples I submitted for the book. I was pretty upset, surprised, and shocked when I received her next email, writing that she was "extremely disappointed" in me for not submitting the proper forms along with the design samples. I sent the filled-in forms to her the next day, but the damage was already done.

They had sent me a PDF of an eighty-page production manual that I had skimmed over, but not read thoroughly. No publisher had ever sent me anything like this before, and I foolishly ignored it, thinking that I already knew everything that they could possibly have to say about book typesetting.

I ended up making a small mistake in the preliminary design samples for the next book design and typesetting project, but they were happy enough with my work that they scheduled me for a third project.

For the first time in my career, the editor sent me the wrong files for typesetting the new book. She sent me an earlier, unedited version of the text. The editor tried to turn the error into an advantage when she realized that a lot of my work would have to be redone, resizing some of the book's photographs in a way that would effect the layout of every page in the book.

I didn't fully understand what she wanted me to do, and when I sent in the new pages I soon received another harsh email, instructing me to return all of the materials and files that I had, and stating that I would no longer be working on the book. I was once again very upset and shocked at this abrupt ending. I emailed the production manager, saying that I could fix the design right away, but she wouldn't budge.

A few months later, having healed from my wounded pride and finances, I was moving into my first condominium in San Francisco, and sent the production manager an email with my new address. I had no thought that they would be sending me more work, but wanted them to have my new address for sending out my 1099 tax form.

I was sent yet another unkind email, detailing all of the mistakes I'd made on the three books I'd worked on. She wrote that these were the reasons she was no longer sending me work. A couple of years later the company was merged with an even larger publisher and all of the people I'd worked with lost their jobs. Even if things had worked out between us, the job would have been temporary. I ended up in a much better long-term position having found other publishers to work for without coming to rely on this publisher as a major client.

Freelancing for the Hippie Commune Typesetting Company

One of my cold-call emails ended up at what turned out to be a hippie commune typesetting company in the

Haight Ashbury district of San Francisco. All of the commune members had assumed new names, each containing exactly three letters.

The company was ranked as one of the top-ten fastest-growing small businesses in San Francisco in the early 1990s. They also published a newspaper depicting their philosophy and polyamorous way of life that was distributed in kiosks all over the city.

The commune had a lot of projects going on and a room full of freelancers like myself, busily formatting presentations, catalogs, and reports for many well-known corporate clients. I was surprised when the commune people ordered take-out from Kentucky Fried Chicken for their lunch, mistakenly thinking that the commune members would all be vegetarian, or at least be eating organic food of some type.

I never made any inquiries about joining the commune and they never invited me in. I only worked for them for a few weeks, until I made the mistake of saying something about "owning" a lot of books. It was the last I ever heard from the commune. I don't know if they were offended by my materialism or unhappy with my work. Or maybe they just ran out of projects.

I was mostly relieved, but a little hurt, when the commune people stopped giving me work, but I had enough other things going on that were keeping me too busy to overly fret about the loss of any one client. My business and future was looking good. I had a steady flow of work streaming in, but still never knew when the next wave of extra-hard work or doing absolutely nothing would strike.

Freelancing for a Another Major Textbook Publisher

Being rejected by the hippie commune wasn't the worst thing that happened to me that year. I lost a great opportunity that turned into my worst-ever book production disaster after I was hired as a freelance typesetter by a textbook division of a major U.S. book publisher with offices in San Francisco.

The production editor in charge of the project had just started with the company and didn't have a lot of experience with book production. She instructed me to retype and format a three-hundred-page best-selling Spanish textbook, offering to pay me $12.00 per page—a good rate for typesetting the book, but not great for having to retype the entire manuscript.

I was rarely asked to type more than a few sentences at a time by my publishing clients—let alone an entire book in Spanish! By now virtually all authors were supplying the text for their books as word processed files.

This book had to be retyped because the previous type-setter had died before she was able to give the publisher the working files for the last edition of the book.

I had some doubts about being able to complete the project on time, but it was too much money for me to turn down, and I eagerly accepted the job. I should have known to turn down the project when the editor told me that I would have only ten days to retype and format the entire book. I don't know if she thought I had a staff that would be helping me out on the project, or if she just didn't realize the full extent of what she was asking me to do.

I got started right away, working at my fastest pace for every one of the ten days I was allowed for the project, and actually finished the job on time. I went to meet with the editor a couple of weeks later when she called me in to discuss the next phase of the project, which would involve fixing whatever mistakes I had made in retyping and formatting the book.

She began by chastising me for the many typograph-ical errors in the text that had been found by the proof-readers. After all the intensely hard work I had put into this project, I found it to be almost comical that she was surprised that I made some minor and easily fixed errors.

One of the best things about being a designer and typesetter is that I'm not the one who is responsible for signing off on books to go to press. There's always a back and forth between me and the editors with some books going into over a dozen revised versions until they are finalized. Book publishers in general don't mind if I make a few mistakes. They realize that it's part of the book production process and that typesetters always miss or misinterpret some of their requests for revisions.

To make things worse, I was unable to complete the project—and fix all of my typos—due to a serious illness. The timing was terrible and it was the end of the road for me with what might have been a great client and a long-term freelance relationship for me.

Freelancing for a Major Music Book Publisher

Soon after my experience with the commune company, I was hired as a freelancer by a big music book publisher with offices in downtown San Francisco. I worked on a variety of different types of projects for them, including some page layout, simple illustrations, and even created the index for a book about a guitar manufacturer.

Although some authors create the indexes for their own books, indexing is mostly done by skilled freelancers specializing in the field. It happened that I wasn't particularly well-suited to making indexes. I lacked the necessary training and skills, and have never even been asked to work on an index again.

My main contact at the publisher was the managing editor, a very nice man who gained points with me for having his young daughter's artwork all around his office. I'm not sure why he gave me so many different types of work, unless he was trying to figure out what I was best suited for. After a couple of months working on freelance projects, he offered me a full-time position at the company. I turned down the job offer, but continued working as a freelancer for a while.

Connecting with a Radical Book Publisher

I was always trying to make contacts and build relationships with local San Francisco publishers in addition to reaching out to potential clients across the country and world. One of my mailings to San Francisco publishers advertising my publishing services made it to the owner of a small book publishing company located just up the street from my favorite hangout, the Caffe Trieste in North Beach.

The book publisher got his start in publishing when he was working at the famed City Light Books on Columbus Avenue in San Francisco's North Beach district. Poet

Allen Ginsberg and bookstore owner and writer Lawrence Ferlinghetti gave him the money he needed to pay for the start-up costs of his first publication, which featured stories and interviews about key figures in the then-current punk rock scene.

The cutting-edge publishing company is best known for a book that featured photographs and interviews of people with extreme body piercings and tattoos. The book was published in the 1980s, long before tattoos became an accepted part of popular culture and was considered quite daring and groundbreaking—the type of book that an established or major publisher wouldn't have considered publishing at the time.

The owner of the book publishing company told me that he had no paying work for me—they worked mostly with interns or did the work themselves—but that I could stop by the office any time, and that he would try to refer me for freelance work to some of his publisher friends and colleagues.

My publisher friend and his wife and partner in the business were always hard at work trying to promote their books, and developing and collecting material for new publications. They ended up asking me to work on a new edition of one of their best-selling books, which they were republishing in a different size than the original—and it had to be completely redone. I don't remember if they had lost the files for the book or if it had been produced in the days before Macintosh desktop publishing and the files never existed.

The book had many design elements, including stylized geometric borders, and hundreds of photographs. Reproducing the pages for the book in the smaller size that would be more appealing to bookstores turned out to be a very challenging project. Trying to match the page breaks and overall layout of the original edition turned out to be a lot more difficult than it would have been to completely start over. Thankfully, everything turned out great with the book and my publisher friends were happy with my work.

Adapting to New Clients and Surviving a Disaster

One of the most important skills that I've learned as a freelancer is how to adapt to the requirements, needs, and even whims of my clients. Every publisher has their own way of doing things and absolutely no patience and little understanding for the fact that others do things differently.

The most important thing I can do for a new client is to figure out their style and ways of doings things, so I can give them exactly what they want—and hopefully exceed their expectations in every way. If I disagree with a client's decisions or requests, I'll do my best to make suggestions and will even put up a fight at times, but ultimately my job is to please the client. The better I can do that, the longer they will be inclined to keep me around.

I've lost some clients who refused to work with me after a first project where I made some mistakes because I didn't understand all of their requirements—or was just having a bad day. I'm usually sorry and disappointed when things work out that way—but often it's for the better as some people are just too difficult to work with.

The worst thing that can happen in my line of work is for a publisher to print thousands of copies of a book with errors that are so bad that they have to destroy the books and reprint corrected copies.

I worked on a complicated cookbook for a large publisher who was one of my best long-term clients. The book was mistakenly printed in black and white rather than in full color as it was supposed to print. They ended up destroying all of the black and white copies and reprinting the books in color. The printer ended up absorbing the cost as it was their mistake in printing the book in black and white, but it was a real disaster for everyone involved and delayed the books coming to market as scheduled.

Even though it wasn't my mistake and the client didn't blame me for anything, it was another lesson in how easily things can go wrong with a publishing project. Things like this always brought me back to the need to grow and diversify my client base, so that I would have enough customers to be able to withstand the loss of one or even more of them.

Almost Freelancing for Ted Kaczynski, Unabomber

My most infamous almost-client by far was Ted Kaczynski, known as the Unabomber, who murdered three people and injured twenty-three with hand-made bombs over the course of many years. A book publisher called me on the phone for what turned out to be a long conversation about a "celebrity" client who had written a new book. We talked about the design and typesetting process in detail, but he didn't tell me the name of the author.

When I told him that I would be available to work on the project, he revealed that the author was Ted Kaczynski, and that he had written a follow-up book to his earlier manifesto. He went on to say that it would take two weeks for the author to receive anything I sent him due to the restrictions of the prison system and that my primary contact would be the murderer's prison girlfriend.

She called me on the telephone the next day and we had a long conversation about how we would work together on the project. A few days later I came to my senses and told the publisher that I was no longer available to work on the project.

There's a certain meeting of the minds that occurs when I work with an author or editor on a book project. I have to figure out how they work and think in order to properly interpret their instructions for text and formatting revisions. Clients are rarely very patient with my errors and misinterpretations of their instructions, so I do my best to get everything right on the first try. I usually maintain a high level of accuracy, but I never take that for granted and always review my work before sending anything out to a client.

A few years later, I searched for "Ted Kaczynski" on Amazon and found that he had gone on to self-publish several books that were for sale on the site. I'm confident that I made the right decision in turning down the project.

Turning Down Freelance Jobs

I'm not in the habit of saying "no" to many of the clients who come to me for help with their books. But if I think there's a good chance that something will go wrong because of the difficulty of the project or something makes me nervous about the client, I won't hesitate to tell someone that I'm not the right person for the job, and wish them good luck with the book.

I had an entirely different reason for not wanting to work on a book of gang symbols and tattoos for an undercover gang investigator police officer when he contacted me. The officer left two long messages on my answering machine saying that he wanted to get together to discuss my working on his book.

Aside from the disturbing subject matter, I was afraid to be seen with him, let alone be involved in the publication of information of this type. I've worked on many books that cover very adult or sensitive topics, including a long series of very graphic erotica, but this particular project had too many red flags for me to ignore.

The Challenge of Finding Regular Work as a Book Designer and Typesetter

My father was an accountant and had many long-term clients that needed work done on a regular basis, whether it was on a daily, weekly, monthly, or annual basis. For me to get a project to work on, someone actually has to write a book and sell it to a publisher or decide to self-publish.

Most books go through many months of editing and rewriting before the manuscript finally comes to me for design and typesetting.

When I send an email to a new customer I don't expect that they will write back to say they have a book sitting there on their desk waiting for a typesetter to contact them. It's not unusual for a publisher to contact me a year or more after I send them my initial contact information.

Something has to be happening for a book publisher to be open to working with a new designer or typesetter, whether it's the recent loss of an employee or other freelancer, or the company's business is expanding and they're seeking to increase their capacity.

Freelancing for Another Division of a Major U.S. Publisher

After my less-than-stellar experience with the Spanish textbook publisher, I was a little nervous when a book production company came to me to design and typeset a series of computer instructional books for another division of the same book publishing company, which was also located in the San Francisco Bay Area.

To get started, the production editor sent me a PDF file of the book cover, which had a variety of graphics and design elements. One of the graphics was a great drawing of the silhouette of a woman's face. I ended up using that image as a border on the inside margins of chapter opener pages (rather than a more typical rectangular shaded area), and everyone thought it looked great.

I had a long meeting at the book publisher's offices with about a dozen people who were involved in the editing, design, and production of the book. I wasn't used to being involved in long face-to-face meetings, and had a hard time sitting through the discussion of every element in the book. I was much more used to and comfortable with just doing the designs and layouts rather than talking about it.

I ended up learning a great deal about book design and typesetting practices and procedures from my work on these books. After the design was finalized they hired me to typeset several of the books in the series, but sent the rest out to another production company. There were about a dozen books in the series, which would have been an overwhelming amount of work for me to receive at one time—although I would have jumped at the opportunity to work on more of the books.

The series did very well and many of the books became bestsellers in the computer book category. This success led to my being hired to design a second series of computer books. Once again, they sent me the already designed PDF of the book cover so that I could use the fonts and some of the images on the interior page design. This series had even more elements that needed special design treatment than the last one and was quite a challenge for me.

Fortunately, I was able to rise to the occasion and the production people at the publisher were very happy with my design work. They sent me a few of the books in the series for typesetting, but once again sent the rest out to a production company that had more people work on the project.

Several of the books in this new series also became bestsellers, which was very gratifying to me and everyone else involved with the project. I was looking forward to more projects to come, but it never happened. I think the production company that hired me to work with them on the books either went out of business, started focusing on something else, or maybe even took an in-house job with another publisher. But I never really knew for sure.

Other Types of Freelance Work

If I had known in advance of all of the struggles and difficulties that I would have to overcome as a career freelancer—some self-imposed and others through no fault of my own—I don't know if I would have had the courage to have taken this path. It's not that things haven't turned out pretty well for me, but there have been a lot of worries along the way that I would not have experienced as a regular employee of a company, or possibly in another profession. I also would have made less than half the income as an employee of a book publisher, most of which are known for the relatively low salaries they pay for the highly sought after work.

Not everyone has the need, skills, or desire to attempt to find freelance work on a full-time career basis like I chose to do. Many people use freelance work to supplement their incomes while they work at full-time jobs, when they're just starting out, or after they've retired from full-time work.

The following table shows some of the different types of freelance jobs in the U.S. and the percent of freelancers in each industry.

Industry	Percent of U.S. Freelance Workers
Art & Design	77%
Marketing	58%
Computers/Mathematics	53%
Construction	52%
Personal Care/Wellness Service	48%
Transportation	39%
Finance/Business Operations	37%
Sales	33%
Education	31%
Management	29%
Healthcare Support	28%
Food Prep/Service	25%
Healthcare	24%
Production/Manufacturing	20%
Office Work/Administrative Support	19%

Source: https://www.zippia.com/advice/how-many-freelancers-in-the-us/

Some Common Freelance Jobs

- Art Director
- Photographer
- Copywriter
- Graphic Designer

- Social Media Manager
- Writer
- Editor
- Proofreader
- Computer Programmer
- Computer Repair and Maintenance Specialist
- Web Designer
- Recruiter
- Salesperson
- Bookkeeper
- Public Relations Manager
- Business Consultant
- Marketer
- Media Buyer
- Artificial Intelligence (AI) Professional
- Data Analyst
- Project Manager
- Videographer
- Desktop Publisher

It's hard to find the line between being a freelancer and being an independent small business. I don't think of my accountant, hair stylist, or lawyer as freelancers, but we all have the same basic business model. One big difference is that all of those professionals have to be licensed to practice their trades.

There are many different types of college degrees and professional certifications for graphic designers, but the profession isn't regulated in any way that requires any type of license or certification to work with customers. Almost all employment listings for graphic designers ask for someone with a college degree or equivalent work experience.

I think many authors and publishers have decided to work with me based on my work experience and client roster, but it has been helpful to tell prospective clients that I have a B.A. in English from the University of Michigan. This was much more important early on in my career—helping to give me some professional credibility with potential book publisher and author clients before I had much actual work experience.

"Desktop publisher," which continues to grow and evolve as a profession, is on my list of common freelancer jobs, but I haven't included book designer and typesetter. Although I know many freelance book designers and typesetters (and editors, proofreaders, indexers, and book coaches), I have my doubts as to whether my chosen field of work will be a viable career path ten or twenty years from now.

Although it gave me a great start in my career, the success and widespread adoption of desktop publishing dealt a death blow to the former career book designers and typesetters who couldn't adapt to the new computer technology. I can easily envision a world where most graphic design and layout production work is done by amazingly skilled AI programs and their well-trained operators, who might be able to produce many books in the time required to produce a single book today.

When I see the type of high-quality illustrations that I can easily create using the current AI image generators, it's clear that what is already great now will only get better. And as always happens, other freelance opportunities will arise in industries that haven't even been imagined today.

It's hard to say which publishing employees and freelancers will be most effected by the coming changes as AI continues to evolve. After most publishers began outsourcing their book production work to India, I never thought that they would start outsourcing the actual editing and proofreading work to offshore vendors. But that's exactly what happened—putting many of my former editor colleagues out of jobs that they loved and thought would go on until they chose to retire.

Hopefully, there will still be many book design and typesetting projects to come that require my human touch, but I expect that a lot more elements of book production will continue to be automated. There have been innumerable changes to the ways books are designed and produced in my forty-year career as a publishing professional. After the invention of desktop publishing itself, the introduction and subsequent popularity of e-books has been the most important innovation.

THE SEARCH FOR NEW CLIENTS GOES ON

CHAPTER 6

LEAVING SAN FRANCISCO

I enjoyed my time living in San Francisco for the most part, and was very proud of myself for have managed to buy my first condominium in the expensive city. But I jumped at the opportunity for change when my parents asked if I wanted to move with them to Los Angeles, where my sister was living with her husband and twin baby girls.

I traded in my small San Francisco condominium for a much larger place in West Hollywood, and had my freelance business up and running in no time at all. The move had absolutely no effect on my home-based freelance business, other than giving me a reason to reach out to all of my clients to tell them of my change of address—and hopefully drum up some new work by reminding people that I was available for work.

West Hollywood calls itself "the creative city," but it doesn't compare to the concentration of artists and writers that I found at the Caffe Trieste and elsewhere in San Francisco. Los Angeles is, of course, home to many screenwriters, actors, and all kinds of creative people in the film industry, but they're a different type than the more bookish people I met in San Francisco.

I was still being kept very busy with freelance book design and typesetting projects from my great book publisher client on the East Coast, and had three or four other book publisher clients that regularly sent me work. The San Francisco Bay Area had a large and thriving book publishing community. There were not nearly as many book publishers with offices in the Los Angeles area. I did my best to reach out through my emails to local book publishers and editors, but had limited success at first.

I ultimately found many clients in the greater Los Angeles area, but since we did all of our work online with the occasional phone call, it didn't really matter where any of us were located. Unlike my time in San Francisco, where I often met face-to-face with my book publishers clients, I rarely met my Los Angeles clients in-person even after many years of working together, so we might as well have been located in different areas. My book publisher clients were used to working with freelancers all around the country—and the world—and didn't really care where I was located as long as I kept meeting my deadlines and doing good or great work.

The high cost of living in California always kept me motivated and hungry to keep building my business. I could have lived comfortably on half of my earnings if had stayed in Michigan, rather than have moved with my parents to California. But then I might never have even thought about becoming a freelance book designer and typesetter at all. In any case, I don't think I would ever have worked so hard keep seeking out new clients without the financial pressures of living in San Francisco and then in the Los Angeles area.

Building and Growing a Freelance Business

I think there are two main reasons that I've been successfully employed full-time as a freelance book designer and typesetter for almost forty years:

1. I never stop trying to reach out to new customers, while doing my best to strengthen relationships with existing clients.
2. I am continually learning everything I can about my chosen field of book design and typesetting, striving to be the best book designer and typesetter that I can be.

Working with publishers to produce books for print can be a complicated process that involves mastering many skills. For the past twenty years, most of the layout work has been done using Adobe InDesign, Illustrator, and Photoshop. Designers need to have a very good understanding of how these programs work in order to produce a book that will adhere to the publishing standards.

www.reiderbooks.com

I've maintained various websites over the years, trying to promote my freelance business by posting samples of my work and doing my best to explain the book design and typesetting process to potential author and publisher clients. I've always created and maintained all of the websites on my own, mostly using the Wordpress platform.

I'm far from being a Wordpress expert, but I've managed to keep the sites going for over twenty years with a little help from a colleague who really knows what he's doing. The site mostly serves to showcase samples of my design and typesetting work. I also have a page with Amazon links to many of the books I've worked on where potential customers can see more examples of my work.

I've experimented with placing Google, Twitter, and Facebook ads but have had little or no success at attracting new customers. I regularly post interior and cover designs samples on Instagram and Twitter and get lots of likes, with some people clicking on the link to my website, but I don't think I've ever gotten a single paying job as a result of my social media efforts.

While this type of advertising and boosting of posts didn't work for me, there are plenty of book design and typesetting firms that do benefit from online advertising. I just have never figured out how to make it work for me. Fortunately, my method of reaching out to customers directly through emails has made up for my lack of success in other methods of promoting my business.

Freelancing for Other Freelancers

I made some changes to my business development strategy and efforts when I moved to Los Angeles. Previously, I had reached out only to management and production people at book publishers. This focus helped me to grow my freelance business and target my marketing attempts, but I always worried that I was limiting myself to a relatively small group of potential customers.

I began reaching out to other freelancers, such as editors, proofreaders, indexers, and any other book production-related people and companies I could find who might be interesting in using my book design and typesetting services. My hope was that some of my colleagues would be able to refer their clients to me after they'd done their work. I also know for a fact that many opportunities can arise from just contacting the right person at the right time. So I had not much to lose beyond my time and efforts, and everything to gain from widening my search for new clients.

One of the best things about reaching out to editors is that a lot of them actually write back to me, either to inquire about my services or at least to thank me for contacting them. My experience with most book publishers was enduring a lot of rejections—or no responses at all—before arriving at the ones that were actually looking for new freelancers, or possibly open to adding me as a new freelancer.

It was a lot easier for me to find new clients when I first started out as a freelancer and the desktop publishing was a new and fast-growing industry. A lot of book publishers were very open to working with me as a freelancer rather than hiring me (or someone else) as a full-time employee.

As time went by and I had to compete with typesetting firms in India, it was harder for me to raise my prices, and in some cases I was forced to lower my prices.

But the competition also made me a better and stronger designer and typesetter and motivated me to always be active in pursuing new clients.

Smooth Sailing for a While

For what seemed like the first time in my professional life as a freelancer, I was enjoying the sweet spot of having more than enough work to keep me happy and fully employed with a reasonably high income. Moving from San Francisco to Los Angeles had absolutely no effect on my business or workflow. The days of my meeting clients in-person or even talking on the telephone were long gone for the most part.

Living in San Francisco and being able to meet people through groups like the Berkeley Macintosh Users Group and BookBuilders West was extremely beneficial to me when I was starting out as a freelancer. Los Angeles has a much smaller publishing community than San Francisco, and I never managed to really connect with as many book publishing professionals here, but I did manage to build some great relationships with local publishers and editors as time went by.

The main downside to the steady flow of work coming in from my book publisher clients was that I was always a little afraid to approach new clients for work, fearing that I might not be able to meet all of my obligations. I have no objection to working hard and long hours on projects, but I am afraid of missing deadlines and the pressure that would come as a result of being behind schedule. Not to mention that being behind on my work would cause my clients to lose confidence in me and take their work elsewhere, which was the last thing they I wanted to happen.

However, as busy as I was, I often had many hours or days between projects, which was great in many ways and enabled me to pursue my interests and just relax at times. But having no work to do also tended to make me nervous and worried as to whether I would ever work again. I compromised with myself by continuing to reach out to new book publisher and author clients, but not at the same pace as before, when I didn't have as much work going on.

Learning How to Make E-books

The arrival and subsequent popularity of Amazon's Kindle and e-books gave publishers another reason to outsource their book production work to off-shore vendors in India. Their workers had the expertise required to produce reflowable ePub e-books, which has been the standard for many years.

Unlike the "What You See Is What You Get" (WSI-WYG) displays used for page layout and word processing programs, the production of e-books requires some understanding of the XHTML coding behind the page display.

Learning to produce reflowable ePub e-books was the biggest technical challenge that I've faced in my freelance career. I got a lot of help from one of my publisher clients, and was highly motivated to learn the process when I was told that I had to learn how to make e-books in order to keep working for them.

After learning some basics, I was able to produce adequate e-books for my publisher clients, but it took me several years to become comfortable and confident in my ability to produce high-quality e-books in a reasonably short period of time.

I never really liked working on e-books because most of the artistry that goes into the print book is stripped away for the e-book, which basically looks like the original Microsoft Word files that authors provide before the pages are designed and typeset into printed books. One of the biggest advantages offered by the e-book platform was that publishers could include the full-color versions of images that appeared in black and white in the printed book due to the high cost of color printing.

Producing e-books requires a lot more technical expertise than working on books for print, and the process was unforgiving. A single tiny error in the construction of the e-book would lead to the file being rejected by Amazon and other sites where e-books are sold. When I first started making e-books, I spent many long and frustrated hours trying to resolve error messages and other issues with the e-book display. It took me a few years of working with the format, but eventually I managed to figure out a great process for making e-books that works well for my clients' purposes.

Aside from taking away so much of the work that had previously been done by U.S. freelancers and publishing services companies, one of the worst outcomes of outsourcing production work to offshore companies was that it significantly lowered the fees that could be charged to produce e-books. My prices had to be competitive with the rates charged by the Indian vendors, where they paid workers so much less for their work than in the U.S.

Creating e-books was much more difficult than working on books for print, and the fees I could charge were significantly less. My fee for the average e-book ranges from $100 to $300, whereas a typical invoice for a print book would range from $500 to $2,000 and sometimes more for longer or complicated books.

As time went by, even the publishers who initially worked with me to figure out the best way to produce their e-books ended up outsourcing their e-book production work to vendors in India. This actually came as a big relief to me and I was very happy to give up the small amount of income that had come from making e-books.

I don't know of many U.S.-based book designers or typesetters that produce their own e-books. I continue to make some e-books for my self-publishing author clients, but I often refer clients to a e-book producer vendor that I work with in India. They do great work for less money than I would be able to charge.

CHAPTER 7

SHUTTING IT ALL DOWN

Things were going pretty great for me when I took decisive steps to compromise my entire financial and professional future. It all started when I signed up for what turned out to be a life-altering photography class at Los Angeles County Museum of Art (LACMA) with a great instructor, whose encouragement helped to convince me that I could become a professional photographer—freelance, of course.

Our first assignment in class was to photograph light. I had a collection of colorful acrylic sculptures made by the artist Vasa Mihich, which were perfect for taking pictures of lights of many colors. I took hundreds of photographs of light shining through the sculptures and then used Adobe Photoshop to combine my images of colored light with regular photographs of people, places, and things.

My instructor at LACMA loved my colorful photographs as did most of the other students in the class. This was all the encouragement I needed to embark on a quest to become a great artist photographer. I became fascinated by photography and spent as much time as possible photographing sites all around Los Angeles and in my West Hollywood neighborhood.

I decided that I was through with designing and typesetting books. I no longer wanted to work on projects for other people. I wanted to create my own artworks through photography and to be a "real" artist and not just a book designer.

What turned out to be my three-year-long obsession with photography left me in a financially precarious position, but I still had my West Hollywood condominium to work out of, and a lot of colorful photographic images to show for my efforts. I had spent thousands of hours working on the images: shooting the original images and then manipulating them in Photoshop, altering the colors and layering multiple images on top of one another.

I knew from the beginning of my foray into photography that I was much better at using Photoshop than I was at using a camera. I managed to create some good and reasonably professional images, but really had very little grasp of the fundamental principles of photography and just a beginner's understanding of how to operate my Canon DSLR camera.

For better or worse, I got a lot of positive feedback on my colorized photographs from many different types of people, and including some artists and designers that I admired and respected. The praise led me to think way too highly of my skills as a photographer artist.

Making one of the worst decisions of my professional life, I contacted all of my clients and told them that I was no longer available for any type of freelance work. This turned out to be a disastrous decision on my part that put me in real financial peril and could easily have placed my entire future at risk.

I did my best and worked harder and longer hours than I had ever done before, producing vividly colored photographs that I thought people might want to buy, and even managing to sell about a dozen prints over the course of a couple of years. I completely enjoyed my time roaming around Los Angeles looking for sites to photograph and then working on the images in Photoshop to edit and enhance the colors.

Unfortunately, or maybe for the better, I completely failed at my best attempts to make it as a professional photographer. It took me many years to rebuild my business to the point where I could stop relying on my savings, and get back to the steady flow of freelance work that I had previously enjoyed. Some of my old customers were happy enough to take me back, but it was a long and hard road, and an experience that I am proud to have survived.

The profound naivete of my ambitions is painful for me to look back on, but I learned a lot about life—and working with color in Photoshop—and became a stronger person in every way.

Some of my former book publisher clients had moved on to working with new freelancers. One of my long-time contacts at a publisher client was laid off from his job, and another client of twenty years had retired during my hiatus. Some of my other contacts had left their positions at the publishers, and as I had experienced before, were reluctant to recommend me to their new employers for fear that it might not work out and reflect badly on themselves for making the recommendation. I understood that my former colleagues were being self-protective, rather than that they were just unwilling to help me.

Starting Over

In my desperate and single-minded focus on rebuilding my business, I spent endless hours searching for the names and contact information of potential new clients. I sent out at least a thousand emails to book publishers around the country with my cover letter, resume, and design samples. I got maybe a handful of positive—or potentially positive—responses. I also reached out to past contacts through LinkedIn and email, trying and hoping to re-establish connections and get some work flowing my way once again.

I had a few things going for me at this point, despite my lack of paying customers. I knew that I could make a good profit on just about any type of book design or typesetting project. My business expenses have always been very low. All I need to run is a Macintosh computer and an Adobe Creative Cloud license and I can turn my time and skills into money.

My first cover letter wasn't very good and received very few responses. I wrote too much about what I had done in the past, rather than what I could do for the client now. I didn't want to draw attention to my age by telling customers that I had been a freelancer since the late 1980s, and have people think that I might not be current with the latest developments in graphic design and layout programs. But I did want potential clients to know that I had a great deal of experience as a book designer and typesetter.

Also, what was once known as desktop publishing was long gone from the book publishing industry and had been taken over by graphic designers, many of whom were educated and trained with technical and theoretical design skills that went far beyond my own. When I started out as a recently graduated English major I saw myself as a having a career ahead of me in writing or editing. I had no graphic design skills to speak of or any real interest in the field.

New Business Prospecting Cover Letter

I've been working on my introductory letter to publishers for over thirty years. When I was getting started in the late 1980s, I went to the library in San Francisco to find names of possible publishing clients from the big reference books full of the type of business contact information that can be easily found today with a Google search.

I loved buying the beautiful Crane's stationery papers that I used to print out my cover letter, resume, and about five or six sample pages of books that I had worked on. Between my regular book work and my reaching out to new publishers, I printed nearly a million pages on my black and white Apple LaserWriter printer. I was forever buying toner cartridges and carrying reams of paper into and out of my office.

Below is the text of the first, and not very successful, email that I sent out when I was first trying to rebuild my business:

I've been working as a book designer and layout artist/typesetter for authors and publishers since graduating from the University of Michigan in 1985 with a B.A. in English. It was the year of the Macintosh computer and "desktop publishing," and my first job was managing a typesetting shop in Ann Arbor.

When I moved to San Francisco two years later my Macintosh skills were very much in demand. I began working as a freelancer for several book publishers and have been at it ever since. My clients have included John Wiley & Sons, Addison Wesley Longman, McGraw-Hill, Rowman & Littlefield, and hundreds of self-publishing authors.

I work on a wide variety of books, ranging from fiction to non-fiction books with complicated layouts, including tables, figures, and photographs.

I'm available to work on the design and formatting of book interiors as well as the design and layout of book covers.

Best regards,
Andrea Reider
Reider Books

The letter had way too much information about my past and not enough of what I can do "now" for my potential book publisher clients.

I had a somewhat better response to the following letter, but was still disappointed by the less-than-great results:

Good afternoon.

I have been working as a professional book designer and typesetter/formatter for print and e-books for over twenty years.

My publisher clients have included Addison Wesley Publishers, John Wiley & Sons, McGraw-Hill, Rowman & Littlefield, National Academies Press, and many self-publishing authors.

You can see design samples at: www.reiderbooks.com.

I'll do my best to bring creativity, accuracy, and the basics of great book design and readability to your books!

Best regards,
Andrea Reider

Things really started to take off when I had the good sense to rewrite my letter yet again, after I saw that the old ones weren't working well enough. The text of my next letter follows, which was much more successful in bringing in new work. I've gotten very positive responses to this letter and many new connections that went on to become long-term clients.

Good afternoon.

I work with authors and publishers to design and format books for print and e-books. I specialize in book interiors but also work on covers.

I'm available to work on just about any type of book, from those that are mostly text to more complicated books with photographs, tables, and other elements.

You can see design samples at: www.reiderbooks.com.

I'll do my best to bring creativity, accuracy, and the basics of great book design and readability to your books!

Best regards,
Andrea Reider

This version starts with "Good afternoon," but I often use "Hello," and will add the first or last name of the person if I have that information. I only use "Good afternoon" if I don't know the name of an actual person at the company I'm trying to reach. These generic letters often end up making their way to the person in charge of hiring freelancers at the company.

Beneath the cover letter I always paste in my resume as an in-line image so I don't have to send it as an attachment that people might be reluctant to download. I also include a link to my www.reiderbooks.com website. My resume includes some career highlights, but isn't close to being a complete list of the many dozens of publishers that I've worked for.

My website has many samples of my book design and typesetting work, along with a page of links to about fifty books on Amazon that people can click on to see additional samples of the book pages. I work on a variety of different types of books, so there are links to children's books, fiction, non-fiction, and other types of books.

Almost Accepting a Non-Freelance (Real) Job

One of my promotional emails came to the desk of a book editor who told me that the publishing department

FREELANCE WORK EXPERIENCE

ACTA Publishing
Design and typeset books, 2020–present

PeopleSpeak
Design and typeset books, 2019–present

The National Academies Press
Typeset books, 2010–present

Rowman & Littlefield Publishers
Design and typeset books, 1999–present

AMG Publishers
Design and typeset books, 2003–2016

Consulting Psychologists Press
Typeset books, 1996–2015

Jossey-Bass Publishers/John Wiley & Sons
Typeset books, 1991–2014

McGraw Hill/Contemporary Publishing Co.
Design and typeset books, 1997–2004

McGraw Hill/Osborne
Design and typeset books, 2000–2002

Addison Wesley Longman
Typeset books, 1991–1997

EDUCATION

University of Michigan
B.A. in English, 1985

of a widely respected hospital in New York was looking for a remote-work book typesetter. I applied for the job in the same way that I sent out all of my emails, with low expectations and a "you never know what can happen" attitude.

The publisher ended up calling me in for an online interview with four employees of the publishing division. I did my best to impress and convince them that I would be a great typesetter for their books. The next day I got a phone call with a job offer. The hourly pay for working thirty hours per week was less than half of what I usually charged and included no employment benefits or health insurance.

Enticed by the thought of finally having steady work, I quickly accepted the job, but my first hesitation came when they told me I had to come to their offices in New York—in the dead of winter—to meet the staff and to undergo a physical examination. Then I started to think of what I might be giving up in committing to work for the lower (but steady) wage and time commitment.

Although I was very tempted by the offer of steady work and how it might contribute to my financial stability, I ended up sending an email the next day declining the job offer. They weren't very enthusiastic when I offered that I was always available to work for them on a freelance basis. I was not at all surprised that I never heard from them again.

It took some courage on my part to turn down the job offer, but it turned out to be a good decision for me. And it gave me some confidence that I had marketable skills that were still needed by publishers and maybe other types of businesses and institutions.

Soon after I turned down the steady job offer, my email efforts began to get some good results, bringing in new clients and a steady stream of freelance work. I never looked back or doubted my decision, but it would have been great to have been able to work for the hospital publisher as a freelancer.

Freelancing for Self-Publishing Authors

Self-publishing authors kept finding their way to me for my book design and typesetting services. The authors come to me through a variety of sources, including referrals from current or old clients and colleagues. A lot of self-publishing authors are referred to me by freelance editors that I reach out to with my emails.

I never felt that I could rely fully on enough money coming in from working with self-publishing authors without also having relationships with at least a few book publishers who could provide me with steady amount of work on an ongoing basis. Although my work with self-publishing authors was less in volume than my work with publishers, I always appreciated the new work, and it was great to be able to supplement my income with this type of work. And there have been some months when I invoiced my author clients more than my publisher clients in total.

I usually charge self-publishing authors less for my design and typesetting work than I would an established book publisher. I would charge more if I could, and it's up to me what to charge, but it's more important to me that I get the work in than that I always maximize my fees for every project.

One of the many good results from working with my self-publishing author clients is that they often asked me to work on their book covers. I was reluctant to ask my regular book design and typesetting clients to send me book cover design work, so this gave me an opportunity to refine my skills and get some experience as a cover design.

Freelancing Again for a Former Publisher Client

I was thrilled and relieved when I managed to re-establish my working relationship with the book publisher I had told that I was no longer available for work when I went off to pursue my failed photography career. Rather than just sending an email, I sent a letter through the U.S. mail to the vice president of production at the company, apologizing for my abrupt departure, and telling him that I was once again available for work as a freelance book designer and typesetter.

Thankfully, he responded right away with a very kind and encouraging email, writing that they would be happy to have me return to work for them—at first on a trial basis—but I was soon able to reprove my worth to them. A colleague warned me at the time that I shouldn't expect the amount of work they gave me now to ever match what it had been before I quit, and that turned out to be quite true.

One of the reasons I had so much steady work from this publisher was that a lot of their books had new editions that came out every year. After I left them, most of the books that I had been working on had been sent to other typesetters, who were now enjoying the steady work. I spent some time waiting and hoping that would give me more work, but I soon returned to sending out more of my promotional emails.

I was still doing my best to attract more freelance work—and had some time on my hands between projects—when I decided to develop a new series of book designs that could be used as templates for books of any size or type. My main contact at the publisher, the managing editor, was very enthusiastic about my new designs, and ended up sending me many books to be typeset using designs from the portfolio of twenty samples that I provided.

Working on the design templates was a great exercise for me and enabled me to expand my design range and break some old habits and ways of doing things. As useful as the templates were, I always enjoy coming up with new designs for books, and always aim to customize the designs to the topic and audience of each book that I work on.

Things were going okay for me when a seemingly insurmountable issue arose that I had absolutely no control over. The state of California passed a new law that changed the definition of contract workers, imposing penalties for companies that did not abide by the new law. The California Assembly Bill 5 (AB5) was an attempt to help the many people who were working full-time for companies as contractors—and were essentially employees—but were receiving little or no employment benefits.

That pretty much describes my freelance relationship with my clients, but I've always been okay with not receiving employment benefits—it's part of my job description. One of the main principles of being a freelancer is that we charge more per hour than a regular employee to make up for our not having the employment benefits.

The lawyers at the publisher notified the production staff that they could no longer hire any freelancers from the state of California. My contacts at the company were as kind to me as they could be, but there was no hope of them being able to send me any work at least in the near future. It seemed that my time working for my great book publisher client had finally come to an end.

Over time I'd transitioned into being a person who was not easily deterred by real or perceived hardships. So I kept sending emails to my main contact at the company every six months or so, hoping that they would reverse their decision or find some way to work with California freelancers.

For three years I was told that everyone still wanted to work with me, but that their hands were tied by the new law. I could hardly believe it when I finally got a positive response. The lawyers had come up with a new contract that would satisfy the state of California and allow me to return to working with the publisher again. Once again, I had high hopes about the amount of work they might give me, but the tide had turned, and I was lucky if they sent me a couple of books per year for design and typesetting.

Back to Freelancing for Another Great Client

I was very happy and quite relieved when my production manager contact at the U.S. government publisher welcomed me back with open arms, when I emailed her that I was once again available for work. They soon started sending me book projects for typesetting on a regular basis again.

The books covered science topics of just about every description, from books about exoplanets and space exploration to more mundane titles. When I first started working for them I thought that their books were all top secret, but when I visited them in D.C., I saw that all of the books were available at their bookstore.

I have a great deal of respect for most of the book editors that I've worked with over the years, but the editors at this government book publisher are some of the best that I've ever had the pleasure of working with. Many of the books are very complicated—requiring a lot of focus on my part—with many elements (footnotes, references, photographs and illustrations, tables, and charts) that have to be typeset exactly to their specifications.

I was more than a little intimidated by some of the editors at this publisher when I first started typesetting books for them. They were so good at their jobs, and I still had some things to learn about the best practices for my own work. I've long gotten over my early fear of failing them, and am always thrilled and appreciative every time they contact me to work on a new book.

Freelancing for Two Entertainment Industry Publishers

One of my emails got the attention of a creative manager who had contacts with the book publishing divisions of major U.S. media and entertainment companies. I enjoyed working on these books, which featured famous illustrated characters from movies and television shows that had to be portrayed in very specific ways, according to the precise and detailed guidelines.

Inspired by my work with these non-traditional book publishing companies, I made some efforts to reach out to other large and small media companies, but I rarely got any type of response from the art directors and creative managers to the introductory emails I sent them. I also started sending my emails and samples to regular graphic design firms outside of the book publishing world.

I kept revising my cover letter in an attempt to appeal to this new client base, hoping that they might be interested in using my services. I didn't get a single new client from my efforts in this direction, and was soon back to approaching traditional book publishers, editors, and book production companies, where I continued to make contact with new clients.

I have no doubt that there are many media companies and graphic design firms that would have been interested in working with me, but I just never figured out how to approach them in the right way or at the right time. There's nothing easy about getting or keeping a book publisher as a client, but it was all that I knew, and my successes and accomplishments in the field always balanced out any failures and disappointments.

CHAPTER 8

BUSINESS BUILDING NEVER ENDS

've learned many hard lessons about how easy it is to lose clients and how difficult it is to find new freelance opportunities. The reward of finding a new client was as high as the possibility of not finding enough work, which was very real and very scary. All of these factors kept me always on the alert and highly motivated to keep building my business and reaching out to potential new clients.

For the first twenty years of my freelance career I worked almost exclusively with large and small traditional book publishers. All of that changed when Amazon's Kindle Direct Publishing enabled self-publishing authors to easily publish and sell their books alongside the books of established book publishers. After so many years of working with only experts in the field, it was a big adjustment for me to begin working with authors who had no experience with or knowledge of the book design and typesetting process.

Traditional book publishers spend months finessing the text and formatting of a book before it goes to press and is published for sale. Some of the self-publishing authors I work with hire their own editors and proofreaders to work on their books, but others send me mostly unedited manuscripts. Some of the editors hired by authors were better than others, but the best of them had usually received their training and experience from working as freelancers or employees of traditional book publishers.

Hard to Maintain Referral Relationships

I spent a lot of time and effort reaching out to many hundreds of the book editing and production companies that work with authors to prepare their books for publication. I ended up getting a lot of referrals from these sources, but there was nothing much that I could do for them in return. Clients usually come to me after the editing is done for their book and rarely ask me for editor or proofreader referrals. It was difficult for me to maintain these relationships without being able to reciprocate by sending them clients.

I have a long-term relationship with a book production company that sends me referrals in exchange for my paying them twenty percent of the invoice total. I tried sending out a few dozen emails to editors offering to pay them a percentage of any work they referred to me for book design and typesetting. One editor wrote back that she was offended by my unethical offer, which was enough to make me pursue other ways to find clients.

One thing I've learned in my many years of working as a successful freelancer is that I have to provide a service that the client needs and values in order for them to keep coming back to me. This also applies to relationships with colleagues. I've referred many clients to other freelancers, but have ultimately stopped doing so when they weren't able to refer any clients back to me.

Book Coaches and Hybrid Publishers

I eventually widened my search for publishing contacts to the growing field of book coaches and a new group of "hybrid" publishing companies. These publishers charge the authors to produce their books, with the clients receiving a higher percentage of the sales than they would receive with most traditional publishing contracts.

I ended up getting a lot of referrals and new work from my efforts to contact people working in the book publishing field, but outside of the world of traditional book publishers. Unlike the steady flow of work that I could expect from working as a freelancer for an established book publisher, most of the self-publishing author referrals had only a single book for me to work on. However, some authors can be quite prolific. I've worked with many who are able to write a new book every year.

Managing Deadlines

My ever-present hope for new work is balanced by my fear of getting overloaded with projects and not being able to finish all of my work on time and to the satisfaction of all. The best way that I know to manage projects with deadlines—some of which are absolutely urgent and others are "no rush at all"—is to start working on projects as soon as I receive the working files from the author or publisher. I wouldn't suggest that anyone or everyone do exactly as I do, but it's a method that has kept me on-time and ahead of schedule for decades.

Not only do I start on almost all projects right away, but I'll often sit at my computer working until a book is completely finished except for my final review and double-check. I manage my schedule this way despite the fact that the deadline may be days or weeks away, and I can't even send the client the completed files until a suitable period of time has passed.

Clients are much less forgiving of any errors I might make if I turn a project in early, with the implication that I may have rushed through the work without spending enough time to do a careful job. Rather than run the risk of looking careless or unprofessional, I often wait a couple of days after I finish my work before sending a client the PDF file for review.

However, my clients are also very appreciative when I turn in my work on their projects ahead of the due date. This gives them more time for proofreading, indexing, and whatever else it takes to finalize the project. I do my best to make my clients look good to their employers and clients by delivering high quality and accurate work on-time or early.

One of the unintended consequences of my way of doing things is that I'm forever putting myself out of work, finishing projects quickly, and then having nothing to do for the rest of the day, or however long it takes for the next project to come in. This sometimes leaves me with the feeling that I have no work to do and may never work again. I try not to drive myself crazy with worry, but this cycle keeps me either hard at work or looking for work most days of the week.

Explaining What I Do as a Book Designer and Typesetter

I grabbed the following text from the front page of my www.reiderbooks.com website. It's my latest and hopefully best attempt to describe my book design and typesetting process. Both self-publishing authors and book publishing professionals may end up reading this, so I try to be specific, while avoiding the use of any industry jargon:

> I typically send three design samples with different fonts and graphic elements to get started, and then make changes or fixes until the design is finalized.
>
> Once the design is set, I begin on the layout of the complete book. I'll need about five to seven days to lay out most books. When the book is complete, I'll send a PDF for review, which the author or editor can mark up with any text or formatting changes or fixes.
>
> Once everything is finalized for the print book, I'll send final PDFs for printing of the interior pages and the cover file if I'm working on that. I typically

send the e-book version of the book within a day of finalizing the print book.

I'm trying my best to be very precise and clear about what I do, hoping to exceed the reader's expectations, and preparing them for what to expect from me.

It's a long way from my early postcards and mailed letters proclaiming that I could do everything: writing, editing, proofreading, design, and typesetting. When I finally figured out what I did best it became a lot easier for me to get my message across to others.

Keeping Current with Industry Standards for Computers and Software

One of the most challenging aspects of being self-employed as a freelancer is keeping up with the ever-changing technology and advances in computing power and software updates. When I'm really in trouble, I'll reach out to a fellow freelancer or other professional for help, but for the most part, I've always done most of my own technical support.

I've always tried to maintain two fairly new Macintosh computers operating in my office at all times. I'm currently using four iMacs (two new ones and two older models) and a MacBook Air laptop. However, I know many freelancer editors, designers, and typesetters who operate their businesses off of just a single laptop.

Difficulties of Working with Some Self-Publishing Authors

I've been hired as a freelancer and sometimes fired by some of the best book publishers in the U.S. and around the world. But I never experienced the difficulties of dealing with disrespectful or even abusive clients until I started working on projects outside of the traditional book publishing world. If anything, almost all of the book publishers that I've worked with have been extremely respectful to me and great to work with.

Most self-publishing authors are a pleasure to work with and the good or great experiences I've had far outweigh the bad ones. However, I've had the unfortunate experience of having to deal with some awful customers, some of whom made unreasonable demands and had impossible expectations due to their not understanding the book production process.

While most authors are understanding of the inevitable errors and issues that can arise when designing and typesetting a book, some authors expect that the first proofs of the typeset book will be perfect. Experienced book publishers understand that I will always make some mistakes or misinterpret some of their instructions or intentions for the book.

I try to prepare authors for what to expect when working with me, and that errors—and fixing them—are an inevitable part of the process. That's why there are so many people working as professional book editors and proofreaders.

An extremely unpleasant and belligerent customer called me "sloppy" and wrote in an email that I was trying to "scam" him because I had missed a few of his hard-to-understand instructions for revisions at an early stage of the book layout. I did my best to just skim over the disturbing emails he sent to me, but I did unfortunately have to read some of his insulting language.

In the cases where a refund is warranted, I won't hesitate to send money back to a client. In my early days of working directly with self-publishing authors I was pretty quick to completely refund a customer's money if they weren't satisfied with my work for any reason or if any conflicts arose.

As my business matured and I became more confident in my own abilities, I began to stand up for myself and refuse to send a complete refund if I had done a substantial amount of work on a project and given my working files to the client. But it was rarely worth the battle. Only difficult customers demand refunds and they can turn quite ugly if they don't get what they want, regard-less of whether or not they are entitled to it.

I still don't know which approach is better. Cheating myself out of the money that I've earned, or dealing with the irate response when I refuse to send an unwarranted refund. I've been called a lot of names and threatened with many kinds of harms to come, but if I do the work and send the client my files, I expect to be paid and will put up a fight when needed to protect my interests.

A small comfort for me when things go badly with a client is that I'm not the only one who has this problem. All of my publishing colleagues have their own irate client horror stories. One book editor that I used to work with changed her entire business model after a particu-larly bad experience with an author of a book about find-ing one's true love.

I've been copied on many emails where I see some publishing colleagues using what I interpret as a servile tone towards their clients in an effort to avoid problems with difficult people. That's just not my style, but I make every effort to treat my customers with honor and respect. I put my best efforts into every project that I work on, and won't tolerate behavior from a client that rises to the level of disrespect or abuse.

Freelancing for Another Book Production Company

One of my luckier emails made it to the offices of a book production company that created and sold book design templates that authors or publishers could use to typeset their own books in Microsoft Word or Adobe InDesign.

They also offered book design and typesetting services using the templates. My job was to typeset the books using the templates (or sometimes a custom design) for authors who didn't want to do the work themselves. I received a percentage of the total invoice.

One of the most challenging projects of my entire career came through an author referred to me by this company. The author was self-publishing a three-volume series of books about rare coins. This was probably the biggest job of my career in terms of the invoice total, and required months of intensive work to complete the books.

As much as I enjoyed working with the book design templates company, the best thing that happened to me as a result of the relationship came when they referred me to another book production company located in the Los Angeles area. I had sent this company several of my promotional emails over the years to no response, so I was very grateful for the introduction.

Freelancing for an Expert Book Production Company

Just when I thought I knew everything there was to know about book design and typesetting, I began freelancing for a book production company that managed the entire publishing process for clients: including editing, design and typesetting, cover design, and helping authors to promote their books.

The firm is run by the best editor that I've ever worked with. She taught me invaluable things about proper book design and typesetting, asking me to fix many of the types of things that would have gotten past even the best of the book editors and publishers that I've worked with.

One of the things that I've learned from my many interactions with book publishers and editors is that they all have their own ways of doing things. Almost all publishers look to the *The Chicago Manual of Style* for the proper rules for book editing, design, and typesetting. But there are still significant variations in styles between publishers and it's my job to figure out and follow each publisher's style.

The book production company kept me busy working on the interior design and typesetting of books for publishers and self-publishing authors, but worked with other designers for the book covers. This was perfectly okay with me as it allowed me to do my best work for the company. I think I'm a very good cover designer, but I've worked with too many great cover designers to consider making that my main line of work.

Freelancing for a Catholic Publisher

I started freelancing with a Catholic book publisher located in the Chicago area after I sent the company one of my introductory emails. The publisher didn't get back to me right away, but contacted me a year later when his long-time book designer and typesetter became seriously ill and had to stop working.

The publisher asked me to design the book covers in addition to the interior design and typesetting. I was a little hesitant about agreeing to the book cover design work at first, but also saw this as an opportunity to gain more experience and develop my skills. I had been working on some book covers for many years at this point, but it was a small part of my business and I never advertised myself specifically as a book cover designer. I told potential clients in my emails that I specialize in interior book design and also work on covers.

Fortunately, the Chicago book publisher was very happy with the cover designs that I came up with, which was all the encouragement I needed to proceed. I found artwork to use for the covers at Adobe Stock Photos and other online sites. I always submit at least three different cover designs using different types of artwork, fonts, and graphic elements. I find this method to work really well as it gives the client a chance to see several alternate covers before deciding on which direction to take.

Sometimes it happens that all of my cover samples are rejected as unusable, but more often than not, the client is happy with one of the options. The best cover designs are usually not created on the first try, and require some back and forth between the cover designer, author, and the publisher. After everyone agrees on which direction to take, I send another round of samples that refine and hopefully enhance and improve upon the original version.

Freelancing for Another Small Publisher

In my constant quest to find new connections, I joined a book publishing industry group located nearby in Pasadena, California, that I found in one of my online searches. My main reason for joining the group was to get access to their member directory, which listed the names and contact information for potential book publishing industry clients.

One of my first emails went to the owner and publisher of a small publishing company, who promptly contacted me and scheduled a meeting to discuss whether we might be a good match. Of course, I was thrilled as usual to have a new potential client, but I would have been even happier if I could have predicted how much I would love working as a freelance book designer and typesetter for this publisher.

The owner of the company had worked as an art director for a major book publisher and was herself a great designer and typesetter. I had a lot of respect for her for having managed to go from working at a publisher to actually being a publisher herself. Our skills turned out to be very complementary—she knew things about book design that I still had to learn, and I was able to help her in many ways with my own book design and typesetting expertise.

CHAPTER 9

MAINTAINING A FREELANCE BUSINESS

As much as I love almost everything about book design and typesetting, it's been a real struggle to maintain enough clients and work to keep my business thriving for every one of the almost forty years of my career. The biggest blow to my business model came when book publishers began outsourcing all or most of their work to vendors in India.

The only way I know to combat the hard times is to be continually working to increase my skills, while reaching out to new potential clients on a regular basis. I used to think that one day I would "outgrow" the need to keep looking for new clients, but it never happened and likely never will.

I haven't been able to raise my rate per page much over the many years that I've been working as a freelancer—and in some cases have actually had to lower my page rates. I would have been out of business long ago were it not for the fact that increasing computer speed and improvements in the software have enabled me to be significantly more productive than I was in the earlier days of my career. I've put a lot of efforts into coming up with methods and systems to increase my productivity, and therefore, my income—by coming up with better and faster ways to do my work.

Accuracy and efficiency are extremely important factors in book design and typesetting. Each time a client sends me a new manuscript for design and layout there's a real possibility that mistakes will occur just about anywhere in the process. I make my fair share of mistakes and sometimes don't understand exactly what's needed for a project at first, but issues and difficulties often arise that are beyond my control.

I've had many authors send me a Word file for design and layout and then a few days later, after I've completed all of the work on the book, they tell me that they have a new version of the manuscript. I think of that like someone bringing their car to a mechanic who fixes all of the problems—and then showing up the next day and saying you brought in the wrong car for them to work on, and then expecting the work to be redone on the second car for free.

Sometimes an author has made only a few changes to the manuscript that I can enter into my pages and salvage most of my work. Other times the author has made so many edits to the text that I've had to completely start over and redo many hours of work—without being able to charge properly for my time. A book publisher would always agree to pay me a fee for redoing work if they ever submitted the wrong manuscript, but author clients don't understand the process and I usually choose to redo the work without charging extra rather than risk upsetting the client and losing the job entirely.

I've lost too many clients due to my making careless and avoidable mistakes. I find that acknowledging my fault and then quickly fixing any errors that I make is the best approach. All errors are fixable before the publisher prints thousands of copies of a book and then notices major or minor errors. Most errors can be fixed easily in the next printed edition of the book, but sometimes an error is so bad that the printed books have to be destroyed and reprinted at great cost to the publisher.

The stakes aren't nearly as high for publishers or self-publishing authors who choose to print their books using print on demand technology, where no books are printed in advance, just as they are sold. As the book designer and typesetter, I'm never the one in the position of having to sign off on a book before sending it to the printer for production. I often wonder how any of the editors I work with are able to get to the point where they're confident that there are no errors in a book and that the project is indeed finished.

Fixing any errors in a book using the print-on-demand process is as easy as uploading a new PDF file to the book sales and printing site, which is usually Amazon, or one of a few other book printing and sales companies that also offer the service. However, most publishers still choose to print their books the traditional way, not using print-on-demand services, because they can produce the books at a lower cost per book and have more control over the entire process.

Maintaining Client Relationships: Keeping Customers Happy

Like any person working at any job, my professional career has been based on the relationships I have with colleagues and customers. I would have gotten nowhere without having developed my skills as a book designer and typesetter, but maintaining client relations is also an art form and is as important as the actual work that I do.

In my ongoing efforts to earn the professional trust and respect of the colleagues and clients that I work with, I always do what I say I'm going to do. And if I'm unable to fulfill a commitment for some reason, I provide a timely, reasonable, and detailed explanation, and hopefully a path forward to have the work completed by me or someone else.

But meeting a client's expectations has never been enough for me to be confident that my publisher and author clients will keep sending me new books to work on. My goal is to be a truly valuable asset to my clients—an essential part of their team. The best way I know to accomplish this is by always doing my best to exceed the expectations of anyone I work with or for.

I always respond to any phone calls or emails as quickly as possible, trying to let at least a minute or two go by before responding so as not to look too eager and available. I strive to provide the highest quality book design and typesetting work possible, and contribute to projects in any way that will contribute to a better book. My clients always appreciate my extra efforts on their behalf, and in turn many have been quite loyal long-term customers—with many relationships measured in decades.

I give clients a choice of at least three different designs for book interiors and covers. Aside from being helpful to the authors and publishers, it also prevents me from feeling hurt or rejected if they didn't like the single sample that I provided. It's unusual for a customer to reject all of my samples and ask me to completely start over, but it does happen. I'm always willing and able to make any changes that a customer requests, but I'll put up a fight if I think they're wrong or making a true or obvious mistake.

I'm very careful to be attentive and responsive to new clients, especially self-publishing authors who aren't familiar with the book production process. But I also do my best to be careful not to make careless mistakes with any of my clients. My mistakes can create extra work for my clients, and can sometimes make them think that I'm not paying enough attention to their projects.

It's not that I'm always stressed out and fearful when working on books—I'm actually quite relaxed and happy most of the time. But I'm always on guard to do my absolute best work for every project that I work on, regardless of the pay or status of the client. I've earned a lot of goodwill from my clients over the years, and most are understanding and gracious when I do make the inevitable or even somewhat careless mistakes.

I'm mostly overjoyed whenever I get in a new project for design or typesetting, but new work also brings some stress and anxiety over whether I can do the work in the time allowed, while managing any other projects that I might be working on. I sometimes turn down projects that may be beyond my skill set, or if there's some other reason that I can't do the work.

How Much to Charge for Services

From the very beginning of my career as a freelancer book typesetter, I've been paid different amounts of money for doing exactly the same work, depending on the client and how much they were willing and able to pay me.

Some of the larger book publishers are willing to pay more than the smaller, independent publishers, but that's not always the case. I've had to compete with book typesetting firms in India since the 1990s, a factor that has prevented me from raising my prices much over the years.

When I'm asked to submit a quote for my work on a new project, it's always a balance between trying to ask for as much money as possible, while avoiding charging too much and risking losing the job. I think I have erred many times by charging too little for my work, but overall I'm very happy with how most projects have turned out. My business expenses are very low and just about any work that I do is profitable, if not always lucrative.

I've also taken on some jobs where I've not made much money for my time and efforts, mostly just to help out people in need, or for a particularly prestigious client or book. I love designing and typesetting books and often do it just for my own enjoyment and to produce samples to show potential clients. I'm more than happy to help out when needed.

Fortunately, I've managed to avoid taking on too many projects that took more of my time and effort than I was paid for, other than in cases where I lowered my fees for a good reason. One of the most important skills to have as a freelancer is the courage and ability to say "no" to some projects. The work you turn down can be as important to your success as a freelancer as the ones that you accept.

Getting Paid

I've been very fortunate throughout my career as a freelancer to have been paid more or less on-time by almost all of my clients. But in running a business with as many different types of clients as I work with, it's inevitable that problems and issues with payments will occur. Sometimes invoices get misplaced or checks get lost in the mail. I've had times where clients that made up a large part of my income suffered temporary financial problems and didn't pay me for over six months or more.

When I work with self-publishing authors, I ask them to pay me half of the total invoice when I send them the initial design samples, and the balance of the payment when I send them the final files for the project. This system has worked out great for me. I've had the occasional dissatisfied author client who insisted on a refund of their 50% advance payment, sometimes due to their unreasonable expectations, and some people are just difficult and hard to please. At times I have lost patience with a particularly demanding or insulting client and I decided to end the relationship with a full refund.

I can't remember ever having to give a book publisher a refund unless they had overpaid me by mistake. Book publishers are tough and demanding customers, but they understand the book production process and know that many rounds back and forth are often required to solve all of the issues that can occur when producing a book.

There's a lot less pressure on me when I work with most self-publishing authors. The stakes are much lower as the worst that can happen is that I lose one or two book projects if the author is displeased. Damaging a relationship with a book publisher can mean the loss of many years of profitable work.

I'm always on top of my accounts receivable—the money for completed work that I expect to be paid within a month or so. Some book publisher clients pay me at 90 days, which is okay with me if I know what to expect. I also keep close track of new projects that authors and publishers have contacted me to work on. It helps with my financial planning and eases my worries about the future when I see that I have plenty of new work coming in.

Reaching Out to Colleagues

I don't know if I would have been able to stay in business for so many years if I hadn't begun reaching out to other freelance publishing professionals and colleagues. I have found it to be very difficult to establish new working relationships with established book publishers, especially the biggest and most prominent ones.

It was also relatively easy to find the names and contact information of other book publishing professionals as there are many websites where I could search for names and email addresses. Unlike most fully staffed book publishers, the editorial and other freelancers actually want people to contact them, so they make it easy to find their contact information.

Aside from the fact that many book publishers continue to outsource most of their work to India, it can be very difficult to find the names of actual employees at large publishing companies. The websites always post a general contact email address but there's no guarantee that my letters will make it to anyone who has anything to do with hiring design and production freelancers.

I find that other freelancers and small businesses are fairly receptive to the idea of referring their clients to me for book design and typesetting after they've done their work on the project. The biggest problem I have in maintaining these relationships is that I don't have enough clients to refer back to them for work. I rarely get requests for editing or proofreading from my clients, but when I do I am quick to refer them to one of my colleagues that has been sending me work.

I place a high value on my relationships with my freelancer colleagues, whether or not they end up sending me work. It's always a pleasure to meet a fellow book publishing professional. I know that they are likely struggling to maintain their client base but that they are also probably loving everything about working with books as I do.

Finding Freelance Work from Online Sites

In my early attempts to rebuild my business after I fired all of my clients, I registered with upwork.com and fiverr.com and actually got a couple of projects from the upwork.com, including one long-term client. It might be that I wasn't very good at promoting myself on the sites, but I felt it was a race to the bottom. Clients usually choose the lowest or lower bids, which encouraged even seasoned professionals to substantially lower their prices. Many of the bids were coming from freelancers located outside of the U.S., which was great for them, but terrible for U.S.-based freelancers forced to live off of very reduced wages.

I also spent some time looking for remote work on employment sites like indeed.com, but that never went anywhere for me. A big downside to working with these public websites is that I was contacted by at least three absolute scammers trying to defraud me, who found my contact information through the employment sites. I caught on to the scams early enough to prevent any real losses on my part, but it was quite demoralizing and upsetting to have been in contact with the would-be thieves.

Make the Most of Your Free Time

Most freelancers take on a lot of risk at some point during their careers. One of the major rewards of being self-employed is that, if you're a little lucky, you'll end up with the reward of having more free time than most people who work regular jobs.

If you find yourself working as a full-time freelancer, but also experience large and small gaps between jobs, I suggest that you find some personally rewarding ways to spend your free time. I have various hobbies and past times that I enjoy, including playing guitar and learning new songs and arrangements. I also follow the stock market throughout the day. It helps to give some structure to my time and keeps me connected with what's happening in the outside world.

Although some of my non-working time is spent trying to reach out to new clients, I always have many hours during the regular work week with absolutely nothing to do. I like to stay productive, which for me includes working on interior and cover designs that I post on Instagram and other sites. I enjoy getting some "likes" and it's great to have the instant feedback on whether people like the layouts.

CONCLUSION

had absolutely nothing to do until 11 a.m. this morning. I rode on my exercise bike, played some guitar, and worked on my book. Then after a flurry of emails, I suddenly had eight new projects to work on. By the end of the afternoon, I'd already finished everything and sent clients PDFs of the most recent versions of their books. As much as I enjoy my free time, I love the challenge of doing a lot of work in a short period of time.

Despite my seemingly endless concerns and worries about keeping enough work (and money) coming in, I always managed to put together a good income from my patchwork of publisher and author clients. When I described my business to a speaker at an employment workshop, he responded with,"you eat what you kill."

I interpreted this to mean that I only made money if I was being paid for a project. Employees of companies have their own concerns, but they do get paid regardless of what's going on with the business, for as long as they are employed.

One of my biggest frustrations has been not always having as much work to do as I knew I was capable of producing. But whenever I felt the anxiety of not having enough work in my office or on the horizon, I was always motivated to keep trying proven and new ways to reach out to potential customers.

When I was first starting out I sent out postcards and fliers saying that I was an editor, proofreader, copywriter, book designer, and typesetter. I had a limited response from this muddled approach and fared much better when I decided to limit myself to being just a book designer and typesetter.

I'm proud of my work as a book designer and typesetter, and as a freelance businessperson. The harsher aspects of trying to make a living as a book publishing freelancer was made easier by the fact that I enjoy just about everything about my job. But my passion for book design and typesetting in no way guaranteed that I would be able to earn enough money to support myself on a long-term basis.

Losing customers is an inevitable part of being a freelancer or any type of business. Because of this fact, it's essential to always be on the lookout for new business opportunities to ensure long-term success. For me, this has meant reaching out to publishers and authors on a continual basis for over thirty years. I find that searching for new work helps to calm the anxiety associated with never knowing what the next day, week, or month may hold.

Any success that I've experienced came from years of hard work, becoming an expert in my field, and taking risks that I would not necessarily have taken if I had fully understood that I might actually fail. However, having given myself few other professional options made the possibility of failure a huge motivation for me to keep trying to grow my business.

I would encourage anyone thinking of following in my path as a career freelancer to think very hard and long about the decision. But if you do decide to take the plunge, you're likely in for the adventure of a lifetime. I derive a huge amount of satisfaction looking back at my freelance accomplishments and take a lot of pride in having done it my way and on my own terms.

I should be getting back to work now. I have a new book in for design and typesetting and am expecting a lot more projects to come. And I've been sitting on what may be a great new list of names and email addresses of book publishing people. As always, I have high hopes, but will persevere regardless of the outcome.

Best wishes and great luck to you on your freelance endeavors! It hasn't always been easy for me, but I would do it again without hesitation, and wouldn't have it any other way.

APPENDIX

INTERIOR BOOK DESIGNS

CLASSIC BOOKS: INTERIOR PAGES[1]

In my never-ending quest to practice and improve my design and typesetting skills—and to promote my business—I embarked on a project to design and typeset the first pages of classic works of literature. The Project Gutenberg website (https://www.gutenberg.org) was an invaluable resource for finding the complete text to classic and out-of-copyright books.

I had experimented with designing my own edition of Bram Stoker's *Dracula* a few years earlier. As I already had the text I needed for my layouts, it was a natural place for me to start. Also, *Dracula* is a great book to work with because of the recognizable imagery associated with the book, including Dracula himself, the moon, wolves, coffins, and bats.

---

[1] All of these samples are available in full color in the e-book edition of this book and online on my website: www.reiderbooks.com. You can also see many of the designs on Instagram at: instagram.com/andreareiderdesign.

I came up with dozens of variations on my designs of *Dracula*, experimenting with different fonts, colors, layouts, and differently colored and patterned backgrounds, until I finally decided to move on to other works of literature. Some of my favorite books to design and typeset are *Anna Karenina, The Tragedy of Hamlet, Prince of Denmark, Gulliver's Travels, The Great Gatsby*, and *Frankenstein*, mostly because of the strong and recognizable main characters.

For me, the process of designing a book is about moving from one concept to another through small or large variations on a theme, some of which can lead to completely new ideas. I particularly enjoyed working on these designs because they were made to be viewed on screen, so I wasn't limited by the constraints of printing an actual book. Most books are printed in black and white due to the high cost of color printing, so I really enjoyed the opportunity to experiment with new color combinations.

These two layouts from the first pages of *Dracula* were some of the first designs that I worked on for my new series of classic book designs and layouts. I hadn't decided yet on my concept of designing and typesetting the first pages of classic books, so these versions of *Dracula* start at different points in the text.

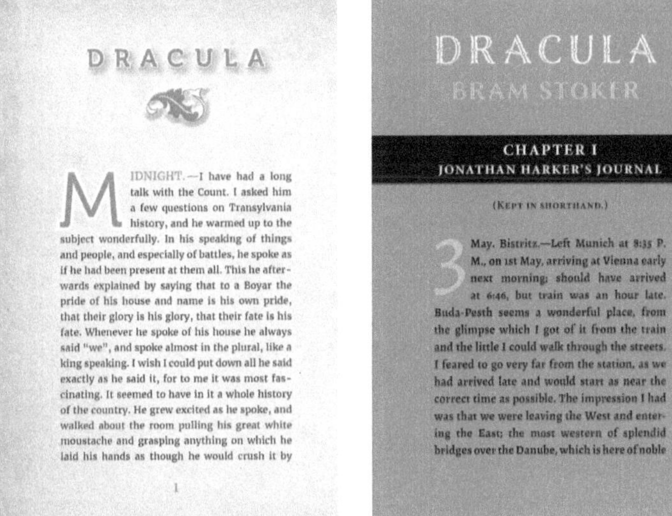

Dracula, by Bram Stoker

These following two layouts of the first pages of *The Tragedy of Hamlet* by William Shakespeare are similar in many ways, but I used different fonts, colors, and printer ornaments. It's unlikely that books looking like this would ever actually be printed unless it was for a specific purpose or audience. The color makes the page more interesting, but it's always easiest to read a book that prints with black type on a white or cream-colored background. I made dozens of variations of *Hamlet.* These are two of my favorites.

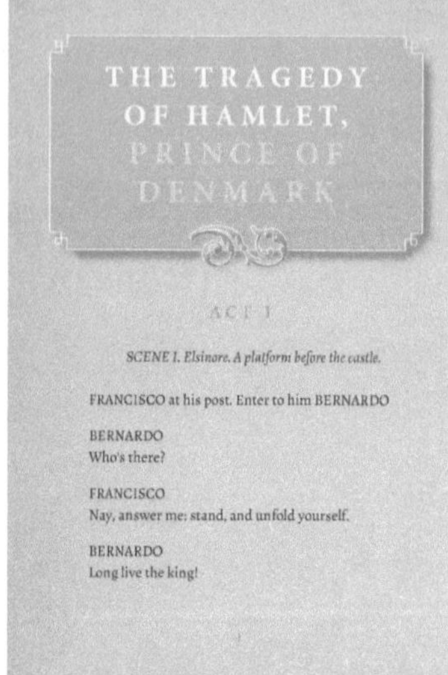 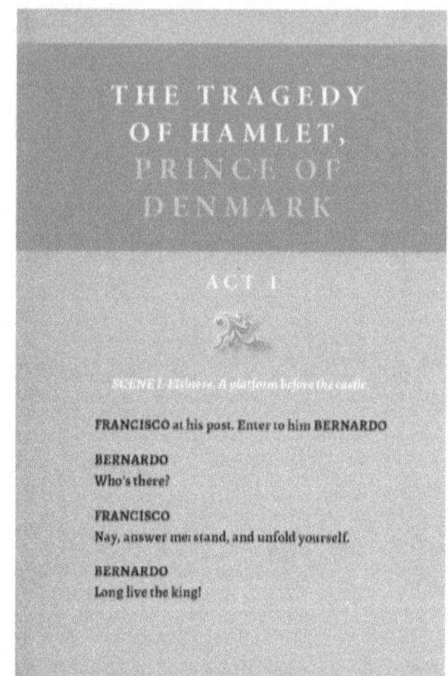

The Tragedy of Hamlet, by William Shakespeare

These two designs for *The Great Gatsby* share the boxed border and gold background. If you've noticed that the left-hand margin of these sample pages are a little wider than the right-hand margin, it's because the inner margins of all printed books are always wider than the outside margins to leave space for the book binding—otherwise the text would fall into the inner folds of the book.

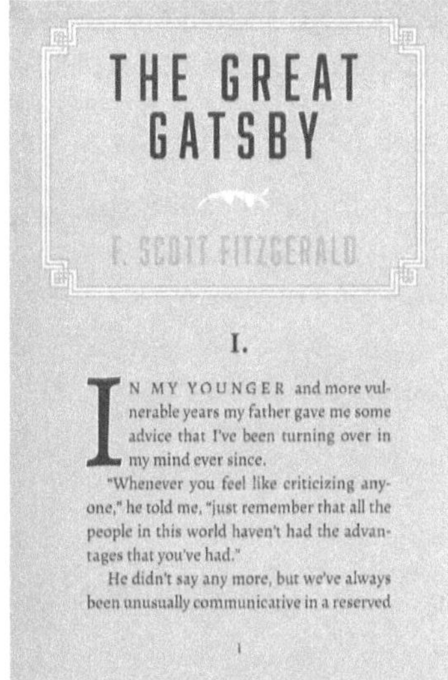
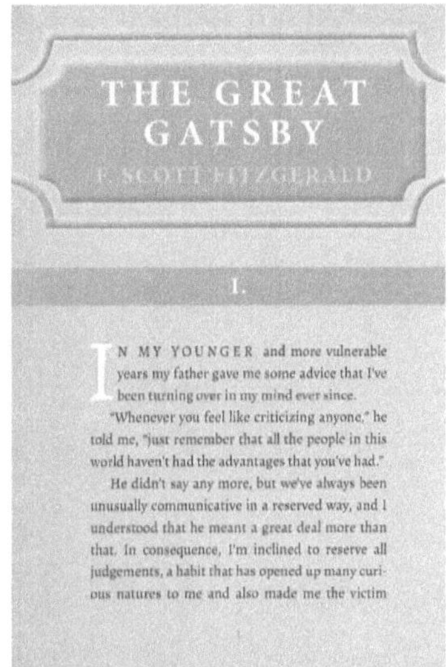

The Great Gatsby, by F. Scott Fitzgerald

These two designs of *Great Expectations* by Charles Dickens and *Gulliver's Travels* by Jonathan Swift use some of the same design elements, but show how color can change the tone of the design. There are an endless number of printer ornaments to choose from. I usually pick three different styles or types of ornaments to show authors and publishers some of the options available.

Sometimes it takes a few rounds back and forth with the author and publisher to arrive at the right ornament for a book. As a designer, it's easy to get lazy and keep repeating designs that worked for previous books. Although I have my favorite ornaments, I do my very best to add variety to my designs, which means that my favorites elements are always evolving and changing.

Great Expectations, by Charles Dickens
Gulliver's Travels, by Jonathan Swift

These two designs for *The Strange Case of Dr. Jekyll and Mr. Hyde* by Robert Louis Stevenson were some of my earlier designs. I hadn't settled on adding the author's name below the book title yet. The type size of the main text is also smaller than in later samples, where I was trying to make the text more readable on screen. The type size is approximately 12-point type with 16 points leading (space between the lines), which is the type size I would use for most printed books.

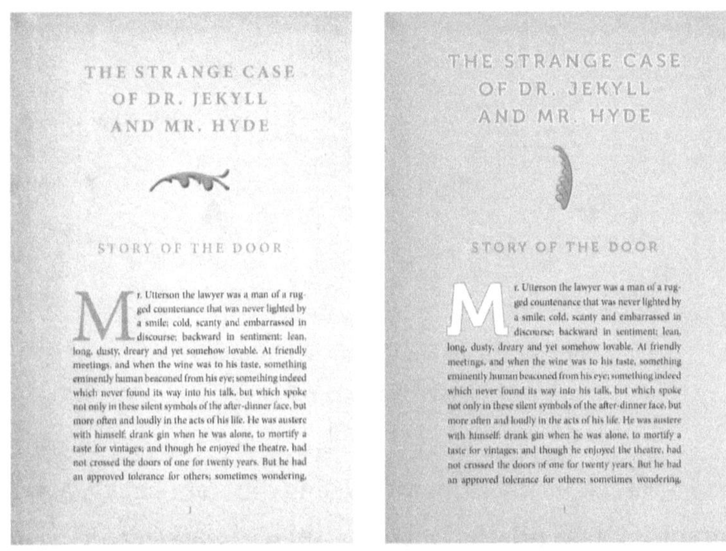

The Strange Case of Dr. Jekyll and Mr. Hyde,
by Robert Louis Stevenson

These are two of my earlier designs for *Frankenstein; Or, The Modern Prometheus* by Mary Wollstonecraft Shelley. My original idea was to add the book title to the first page of the book as in these samples, but then I realized that I needed to add the author names as well.

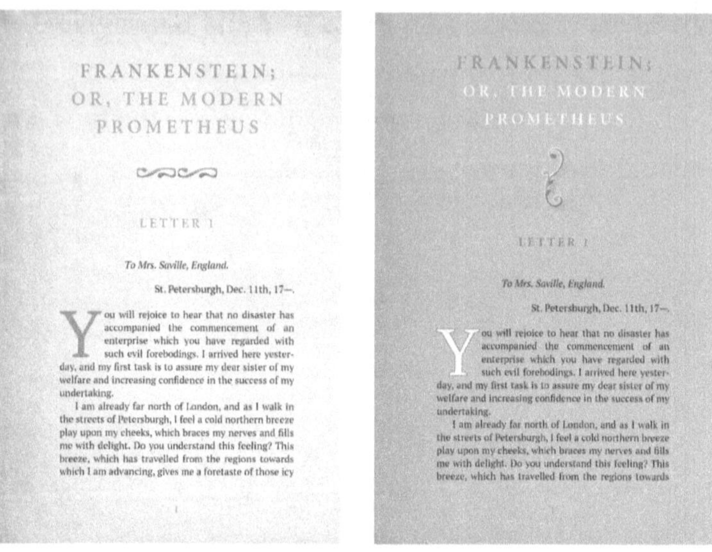

Frankenstein: Or, the Modern Prometheus,
by Mary Wollstonecraft Shelley

I was experimenting with using different background graphics behind the text for these *Frankenstein* page designs. There's plenty of room to add the author name above or below the book title without having to reduce the type size by much.

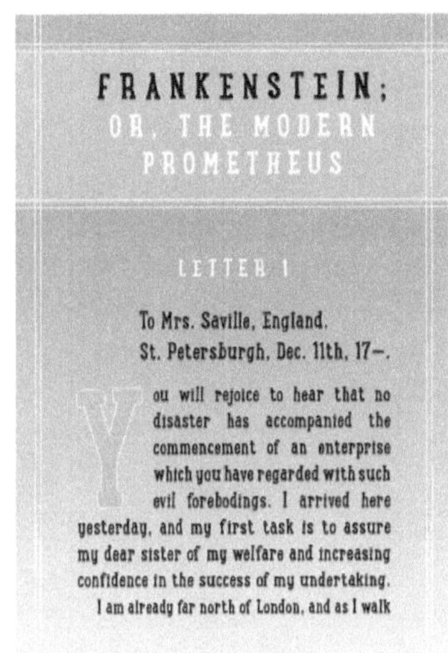
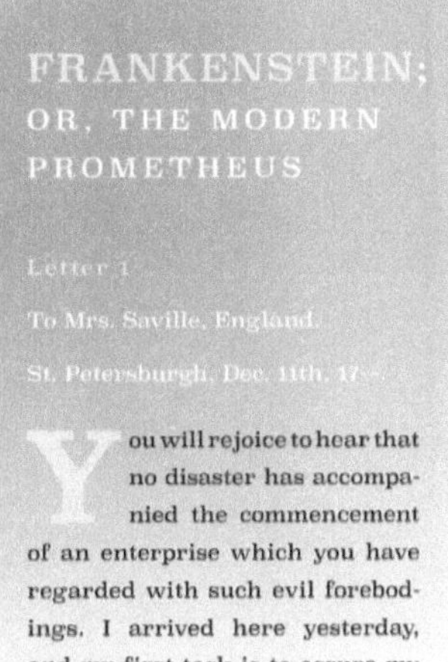

Frankenstein: Or, the Modern Prometheus,
by Mary Wollstonecraft Shelley

When authors and publishers hire me to design and typeset their books, I do my best to present the material in the most readable and attractive form that is appropriate to the topic and audience. I wouldn't expect many people to pick up one of the books I've worked on and marvel at the perfect margins or spend much time looking at the well-chosen printer ornaments or borders. My purpose is to get people to read the book, and hopefully enjoy the well-balanced pages and beautiful typefaces along the way.

ABOUT THE AUTHOR

Andrea Reider graduated from the University of Michigan with a B.A. in English in 1985, which was the beginning of the Macintosh computer and desktop publishing revolution. A first job at a typesetting shop in Ann Arbor led to a lifelong career as a freelance book designer and typesetter for a wide variety of book publishers and authors.

After moving to San Francisco in the late 1980s, Andrea connected with several major book publishing clients. Working as a freelancer proved to be a perfect match for Andrea's ambitions and skills, leading to a very happy and purpose-filled life and career.

www.reiderbooks.com